D1624657

HEAVENLY SUPPER

FULVIO TOMIZZA

HEAVENLY SUPPER

THE STORY OF
MARIA JANIS

Translated by
ANNE JACOBSON
SCHUTTE

THE UNIVERSITY OF CHICAGO PRESS
Chicago and London

FULVIO TOMIZZA is the author of twenty-two books and three plays. His honors include the Premio Strega, Italy's most distinguished literary award, and the Austrian State Prize for European Literature. *Heavenly Supper* is the first of his works to appear in English.

The University of Chicago Press, Chicago 60637
The University of Chicago Press, Ltd., London
© 1991 by The University of Chicago
All rights reserved. Published 1991

00 99 98 97 96 95 94 93 92 91   5 4 3 2 1

Originally published as *La finzione di Maria,* © 1981
by RCS RIZZOLI LIBRI S.p.A., Milano

Tomizza, Fulvio, 1935–
    [Finizione di Maria. English]
Heavenly supper : the story of Maria Janis / Fulvio Tomizza :
    translated by Anne Jacobson Schutte.
                    p.   cm.
          Translation of: La finzione di Maria.
          Includes bibliographical references.
      1. Janis, Maria, 17th cent.   2. Catholics—Italy—Venice—
Biography.   3. Venice (Italy)—History—1508–1797.   4. Lord's
    Supper—Miracles.   5. Inquisition—Italy—Venice.   I. Title.
             BX4705.J3375T6513   1991
             945′.3107′092—dc20
[B]   91–14297
                                                                CIP
          ISBN 0–226–80789–4

Printed in Mexico

And if we were to recount many other things that happened to us inquisitors in the course of our duties, we would win the admiration of readers everywhere. However, since self-praise is no recommendation, we shall pass over them in silence, so as not to gain a reputation for boastfulness.

Heinrich Institor (Krämer) and Jakob Sprenger, *Malleus Maleficarum* (*The Witches' Hammer*), part II, question 1, preface.

CONTENTS

TRANSLATOR'S INTRODUCTION

Fulvio Tomizza, the author of twenty-two books and three plays,[1] is well known in Italy, where he has achieved critical recognition and a large and enthusiastic following among readers. Several of his books have won prizes; one of them, *La miglior vita,* earned the most distinguished Italian literary award, the Premio Strega. Almost all of them have been translated into at least one other European language, *La miglior vita* into ten. *Heavenly Supper: The Story of Maria Janis* (original title: *La finzione di Maria*) is the first of his works to appear in English.

Tomizza has characterized himself as "a man on the border" between two nations, Italy and Yugoslavia, and two cultures. Born in 1935 in Materada, a village on the Istrian peninsula about twenty-five miles south of Trieste, he grew up in a family of mixed origins. On his father's side, he is descended from Albanian Christians who immigrated to Istria in the seventeenth century to escape the Turks and became fully Italianized; on his mother's side, his heritage is partly Slavic. From the end of World War I until 1954, Istria was part of Italy. Its population, however, was divided: on the coast, Italian-oriented and Italian-speaking (the Istrian dialect is closely related to Venetian); in

1. Here I list only the titles and dates of original publication; many have been or are about to be reissued. The first two categories into which I have divided them, for reasons that will become apparent shortly, are my own; in Italian critical terminology, both fall under the heading *narrativa* (as opposed to *saggistica*). Novels and collections of short stories: *Materada* (1960), *La ragazza di Petrovia* (1963), *La quinta stagione* (1965), *Il bosco della acacie* (1966), *L'albero dei sogni* (1969), *La torre capovolta* (1971), *La città di Miriam* (1972), *Dove tornare* (1974), *La miglior vita* (1977), *L'amicizia* (1980), *Ieri, un secolo fa* (1985), *Poi venne Cernobyl* (1989). Historical studies: *La finzione di Maria* (1981), *Il male viene dal Nord: Il romanzo del vescovo Vergerio* (1984), *Gli sposi di Via Rossetti: Tragedia in una minoranza* (1986), *Quando Dio uscì di chiesa: Vita e fede in un borgo istriano del Cinquecento* (1987), *L'ereditiera veneziana* (1989), *Fughe incrociate* (1990), *L'abate Roys e il fatto innominabile* (1991). Books for children: *Trick: Storia di un cane* (1975), *La pulce in gabbia* (1979), *Il gatto Martino* (1983). Plays: *Vera Verk* (1963), *La storia di Bertoldo* (1969), *L'idealista* (1976).

the interior, Slovene-speaking near Trieste and Croatian-speaking on the rest of the peninsula.

During the twenty years of Mussolini's rule and the final stages of World War II, tensions between these two groups grew, primarily because of the Fascist regime's policy of Italianizing the entire population but also because to a certain extent linguistic and cultural differences were paralleled by economic differences. (The Italians tended, or at least were perceived, to be more prosperous.) Once the war was over and Istria was provisionally divided between Italy and Yugoslavia, hostility between the peninsula's Slavic and Italian inhabitants, hitherto muted, broke out into open antagonism. Tomizza's father was one of the victims. A landowner and merchant of modest means, philo-Italian but not politically active, he was arrested and jailed. Not long after his release, he died prematurely of tuberculosis.

At the time of his father's death, Tomizza had just completed his secondary education. Seeing the political handwriting on the wall, Italian Istrians had to make up their minds whether to cast their lot with Yugoslavia or to move across the new border (established by the bilateral London Memorandum of 1954) into Italy. Tomizza's mother and older brother opted immediately for the second alternative. He, however, decided to remain in his homeland, and he set off for the University of Belgrade to study literature. After a few months, he changed his mind and settled in Trieste. For twenty years he worked there and in Rome as a journalist for RAI, the Italian state radio-television network, writing in his spare time. His literary production during that period testifies to his impassioned and disciplined approach to what he has always considered his major vocation. Although he holds Italian citizenship and maintains his primary residence in Trieste, since 1981 he has been able to spend at least half the year near his native village in Istria in a small stone house once inhabited by peasants. There he does most of his writing.

In his works published before *La finzione di Maria,* Tomizza's main theme was the conflict between two cultures, of which he is a product and in a certain sense a victim. Unlike most victims, he has not taken sides. On the contrary, in all his works concerning Istria and its ordeal, as well as in his public activities and statements, he has promoted the transcending of old differences and hatreds. Tomizza's concentration on "the matter of Istria" has led some to dismiss him as a regional writer. In fact, the term is as inadequate a category for him as it would be for William Faulkner. As his readers and most discerning critics can testify, he addresses universal questions raised in all significant works of literature: hate and love, pain and pleasure, incomprehension and understanding.[2]

With *La finzione di Maria,* Tomizza entered a territory new to him, historical narrative. As he explains in the Afterword, he had made a preliminary reconnaissance in *La miglior vita,* but there a historical document served as a stimulus to an imaginative re-creation. *La miglior vita* can properly be termed a novel. In contrast, *La finzione di Maria*—like six other books which Tomizza has written since—is, as I shall demonstrate, a historical work.

This is hardly the place for a long theoretical discussion of narrativity. Instead, let me offer some observations about fictional and historical narrative that might be termed "practical criticism"—the sort that is most congenial, I think, to the majority of practicing historians and may interest amateurs of history as well.

What distinguishes fictional narrative from historical narrative? For some, there is a single, simple answer to this question: novelists write fiction and historians write history. Tomizza is a novelist; ergo, the books he writes are novels. Publishers take it for granted that the public expects novelists to write novels accessible to all and pleasant to read, and historians and other academicians to produce heavy tomes intended exclusively for the edification of their colleagues and students. With a few exceptions—biographies of famous people, popularized studies of major events such as the French Revolution and World War II—"real" works of history are assumed to be of no interest to the "general reader." That is why the publisher of *La finzione di Maria* put the word *romanzo* (novel) on the dust jacket. Three years later, another publisher, issuing Tomizza's study of Pier Paolo Vergerio, promoted *romanzo* to the status of subtitle.

Some recent evidence—the success of Carlo Ginzburg's *The Cheese and the Worms,* Natalie Zemon Davis's *The Return of Martin Guerre,*

2. The fullest critical study of Tomizza's work previous to *La finzione di Maria* is Marco Neirotti, *Invito alla lettura di Fulvio Tomizza* (Milan: Mursia, 1979).

Judith Brown's *Immodest Acts,* and Gene Brucker's *Giovanni and Lusanna*[3]—suggests, however, that as far as the general public is concerned, the statement "novelists write fiction, historians write history" is no longer an eternal truth. I cannot count the number of "general readers," both students and adults, who have told me after reading one of these books, "It reads just like a novel! I couldn't put it down! Can you recommend any other history books like that?"

"It reads just like a novel!": that is the heart of the matter. A major characteristic of the four works I have just mentioned is their focus on an individual or a small group of people. In one sense, the protagonists could be termed "ordinary people"—as opposed to rulers, generals, or figures who achieved renown among their contemporaries through their accomplishments in some other field. For this reason accounts of these "ordinary" lives have a special attraction for ordinary people of the late twentieth century. But in another sense, the lives are "extraordinary," or, as their contemporaries put it, "prodigious." These individuals emerged for a moment from the anonymous mass in the lower orders of society because they did something that was defined by the authorities as a crime. Thus their names were entered in judicial records (and in rare instances, such as the case of Martin Guerre, also in contemporary accounts). Having rediscovered in the transcripts of court proceedings those brief moments of notoriety, historians have re-created them, thereby transmuting them into historical fame. The term coined by its practitioners for this kind of historical study is "microhistory."

Some critics of microhistory have objected that the very extraordinariness of its protagonists disqualifies them as subjects of real, significant historical writing. What, they ask, can we learn from such "extreme cases" about the lives of common people in the past? Are Menocchio, Martin Guerre, Benedetta Carlini, and Lusanna really anything more than isolated curiosities? And are the necessarily conjec-

3. Carlo Ginzburg, *Il formaggio e i vermi: Il cosmo di un mugnaio del '500* (Turin: Einaudi, 1976)—English translation by John and Anne Tedeschi, *The Cheese and the Worms: The Cosmos of a Sixteenth-Century Miller* (Baltimore and London: Johns Hopkins University Press, 1980). Natalie Zemon Davis, *The Return of Martin Guerre* (Cambridge, Mass.: Harvard University Press, 1983). Judith C. Brown, *Immodest Acts: The Life of a Lesbian Nun in Renaissance Italy* (New York and Oxford: Oxford University Press, 1986). And Gene Brucker, *Giovanni and Lusanna: Love and Marriage in Renaissance Florence* (Berkeley, Los Angeles, and London: University of California Press, 1986).

tural reconstructions of their life histories from biased and incomplete court records anything more than trivial pursuits, debasements of the noble art and craft of historical writing into something resembling a novel in one of its "lowest" forms, the detective story?[4]

Summarizing the responses (in my view fully persuasive) made to these objections by those who practice and analyze microhistory would take us too far afield.[5] From the critical epithets employed by the opponents of microhistory, however, we can obtain some valuable clues about the similarities, as well as some differences, between fictional and microhistorical narrative. Notice that the critics' terms are remarkably similar to lay readers' laudatory comments. "Novels/detective stories": that is precisely what microhistories are. They feature a limited number of protagonists, with specified antagonists (the judicial authorities) in hot pursuit. They are full of suspense. Did the alleged perpetrators really do it? When, how, and why? How do the prosecutors go about tracking them down? Are the witnesses, particularly the relatives and neighbors of the accused, antagonists or accomplices? Will the "criminals" be able to mount any kind of defense in court, and if they are found guilty, what will the sentence (and the rationale behind it) be?

Although microhistorians, like writers of detective novels, concern themselves with a restricted cast of characters, they cannot and do not treat them in isolation. In order to get the plot off the ground, keep it moving, and bring it to a conclusion, they need to create, or re-create, the milieux in which the characters lived and operated.

4. See, for example, Paola Zambelli, "Uno, due, tre, mille Menocchio," *Archivio storico italiano* 137 (1979): 51–90; Robert Finlay, "The Refashioning of Martin Guerre," *American Historical Review* 93 (1988): 553–71; and Steven Ozment, *Three Behaim Boys: Growing Up in Early Modern Germany* (New Haven and London: Yale University Press, 1990), xi–xiii.

5. See, for example, Carlo Ginzburg, "Clues: Roots of an Evidential Paradigm," in his *Clues, Myths, and the Historical Method,* trans. John and Anne C. Tedeschi (Baltimore and London: Johns Hopkins University Press, 1989), 96–125; Ginzburg, "Prove e possibilità: In margine a *Il ritorno di Martin Guerre* di Natalie Zemon Davis," in Natalie Zemon Davis, *Il ritorno di Martin Guerre* (Turin: Einaudi, 1984), 131–54; Natalie Zemon Davis, "'On the Lame,'" *American Historical Review* 93 (1988): 572–603; Ottavia Niccoli, *Prophets and People in Renaissance Italy,* trans. Lydia G. Cochrane (Princeton: Princeton University Press, 1990), xvii–xviii; Edward Muir, "Introduction: Observing Trifles," in *Microhistory and the Lost Peoples of Europe: Selections from* Quaderni storici, ed. Edward Muir and Guido Ruggiero, trans. Eren Branch (Baltimore and London: Johns Hopkins University Press, 1991).

Only by so doing can they answer the "who," "what," "when," "how," and "why" questions that the actions of the protagonists and the reactions of the onlookers and antagonists raise. These milieux are not the world of anonymous masses and vast impersonal forces shaped or channeled by a few world-historical figures—which according to some is the only proper territory of the historian—but rather stages circumscribed by the demands of the "stories" as interpreted by their creators. Not *histoire totale,* then, but rather *histoire problème.*[6]

Most stories, whether fictional or historical, have a beginning, a middle, and an end. In neither case is the trajectory dictated in advance by the hands of a clock or the pages of a calendar. The creators of stories must decide whether to proceed in strict chronological order or in some other fashion, whether to interpolate flashbacks, and when to slow down or speed up the action. Here historians are in very much the same kind of control as novelists. The boundaries of choice, though they certainly exist, are wide and flexible.

The same is the case with authorial presence. Historians, just like novelists, can elect to keep themselves entirely out of the picture, thus attempting to draw attention away from or even disguise the fact that they themselves, by representing the story, have made it. At the other extreme, they can lay all their cards on the table, speaking directly to their readers and sharing with them their reasons for having decided to tell the story, their difficulties in interpreting their material, their perplexities about how to proceed, and their reflections about the "moral" of the stories—that is, the relevance to the producers and consumers thereof in the late twentieth century.[7]

Particularly when they adopt the second approach, the historians' "I"'s are not the eyes of God or the supposedly removed and therefore "objective" vantage point of natural and social scientists (whose prose, it may be noted, is characterized by the virtual absence of the first-person singular pronoun and the predominance of the pas-

---

6. See J. H. Hexter, "Fernand Braudel and the *Monde Braudellien* . . . ," *Journal of Modern History* 44 (1972): 480–539. The analysis that follows is much indebted to another article by Hexter, "The Rhetoric of History," in his *Doing History* (Bloomington and London: Indiana University Press, 1971), 15–76.

7. The best example I know of such "full disclosure" is the account of a seminar project undertaken at the University of Bologna: Carlo Ginzburg and Adriano Prosperi, *Giochi di pazienza: Un seminario sul "Beneficio di Cristo"* (Turin: Einaudi, 1975).

sive voice). On the contrary, "principal investigators" who are historians pursue possibilities rather than certainties, the most plausible among several alternative explanations. Their prose is studded with conjectural signs: interrogatives, conditional and subjunctive constructions, adverbs such as "perhaps." They are well aware that they and their readers can never know for sure "how it really happened." Although they stop short of complete relativism—after all, there are ways of distinguishing "better" (or more likely) from "worse" (or less likely, even entirely implausible) explanations—they recognize that conducting full-scale laboratory tests of their hypothetical reconstructions, in which variables would be measured and rigorously controlled, is not within their powers.

In many respects, then, microhistorians and other historians who tell stories are engaged in an enterprise similar to that of novelists, and they use several of the same means to achieve their ends. I do not mean to suggest, however, that there are no differences whatever between fictional and historical narratives. The former can spring to a very large extent, though never totally, from the mind of their creators. The latter are based on documents, traces of the past in written or nonwritten form. Furthermore, they manifest their fidelity to the historical record by making direct reference to the documents, both in precise and judiciously marshaled direct quotations and in accurate paraphrases and summaries of them. So that readers, if they choose to do so, can judge whether the conjectural reconstruction of historical stories is plausible, they are given full information about where the sources on which the stories are based may be found. That is, historical narratives include some kind of documentary apparatus: notes and/or an essay on sources. A final characteristic of historical, as distinguished from fictional, narratives is the inclusion of some reference to "the state of the art": acknowledgment, or in some instances refutation, of what previous historians have discovered that bears on the subject.

Because it is solidly grounded in a document, the record of a trial conducted by the Venetian Inquisition, *Heavenly Supper* resembles a microhistory written by a professional historian. The resemblance is more than superficial. Tomizza asks all the questions historians ask. Going beyond the trial record, he seeks to evoke the broader milieu in which his cast of characters operated. His interest and sympathy undoubtedly lie on the side of the defendants, but he does not turn the prosecutors into cardboard villains. In other words, he is operating as a historian.

Tomizza's narrative strategies also come from the tool kit common to novelists and historians. Like most microhistorians, he chooses to begin as the trial opens rather than at some earlier point in time, such as Maria Janis's birth. He then deploys his story in a rather complex fashion that bears a close resemblance to the narrative scheme Natalie Davis would later adopt: alternating a chronological account of the judicial proceedings with analyses of each protagonist's previous life history.[8] His authorial stance is clearly of the second type identified above. Both in the body of the book and in the Afterword, he is present in the first person, admitting his doubts and difficulties and reflecting on the immediate and long-term significance of the story he is telling. He employs the full arsenal of conjectural signs to indicate that "this is the way it may have been" at points where he has no means of knowing for certain that "this is the way it was." As he thinks his way into the minds and hearts of his protagonists at critical junctures of their lives, he does no more and no less than what historians must do if they are to make sense of the past.

Tomizza refrains from embroidering upon the historical record. This book contains no invented incidents and only one fragment of invented dialogue, clearly identified as such.[9] Instead, he gives his characters ample but not excessive opportunity to speak for themselves in their own words.[10] His interest in and sensitivity to language—and above all, his intimate knowledge of Venetian and other regional dialects employed in the Venetian Republic—are among the greatest strengths he brings to the microhistorical enterprise.

Unlike a historical novel, *Heavenly Supper* is adequately documented. Tomizza specifies his main source and supplies references to

8. The resemblance is entirely coincidental. As she explains in the preface to *The Return of Martin Guerre,* Davis devised this organizational scheme after she had participated in a fictional (cinematographic) reconstruction of the story that proceeds in more or less chronological order.

9. "With all these mouths I have to feed, I'd like to learn how to get along without eating!" Chapter 6, p. 44.

10. Natalie Zemon Davis has shown particular interest in this aspect of historical writing. See especially her *Fiction in the Archives: Pardon Tales and Their Tellers in Sixteenth-Century France* (Stanford: Stanford University Press, 1987).

other works he has consulted. Because the manuscript of the trial is unpaginated, footnoting every quotation, paraphrase, and summary is not feasible; readers who wish to check on his accuracy can easily do so by following the chronological indications he provides. What might appear to be a paucity of references to "the state of the art" reflects the fact that when the book was published, the products of sophisticated research on inquisitorial procedure were just beginning to appear, microhistory was in its infancy, and the fascinating phenomenon of pretense of sanctity had barely been identified.[11] In 1981, there was not much directly relevant scholarship to cite.

Thus *Heavenly Supper,* a fine example of the convergence of fictional and historical narrative, can be properly termed a microhistory. Thanks to a publisher willing to take chances by questioning the conventional wisdom about genres, Anglophone connoisseurs of historical narrative, both professionals and amateurs, who did not know of or were unable to read it in the original now have the opportunity to do so. I wish to express my gratitude to Douglas Mitchell and Jo Ann Kiser of the University of Chicago Press, to my colleagues Michael Hittle and Peter Fritzell, to William Schutte, and above all to Fulvio Tomizza for their invaluable assistance in my efforts to make Maria Janis, her friends, and her antagonists speak English.

Anne Jacobson Schutte
Venice
Ferragosto 1990

11. The only previous studies I know of are Giuseppe Paladino, "Suor Cristina Rovoles creduta santa e il suo processo," *Archivio storico siciliano* n.s. 36 (1911): 113–25; Giovanni Romeo, "Una 'simulatrice di santità' a Napoli nel '500: Alfonsina Rispola," *Campania sacra* 8–9 (1977–78): 159–218; and Luisa Ciammitti, "One Saint Less: The Story of Angela Mellini, a Bolognese Seamstress (1667–17[?])" (1979), trans. Margaret A. Gallucci, in *Sex and Gender in Historical Perspective: Selections from* Quaderni Storici, ed. Edward Muir and Guido Ruggiero (Baltimore and London: Johns Hopkins University Press, 1990), 141–76.

NOTE ON THE TRANSLATION

This translation, I hope, belies the old Italian adage "*Tradurre è tradire* [To translate is to betray]." With Fulvio Tomizza's encouragement, I have attempted to capture the sense and spirit of the Italian, rather than to render it in a painfully literal fashion. In the transcript of the trial (Venice, Archivio di Stato, Sant'Uffizio, busta 110), which I had before me as I prepared the translation, the inquisitor's questions are recorded in the third person, defendants' and witnesses' responses in the first person—a typical practice of Inquisition notaries. To achieve syntactical consistency in direct quotations, I have silently altered pronouns and verbs.

Tomizza could assume familiarity on the part of his original audience with Italian geography, Catholic theology and practice, and other matters. In order to provide information that, in my judgment, readers of the English edition need, I have supplemented some of the author's notes and supplied others. Square brackets in the notes indicate translator's additions.

I
THE END OF A JOURNEY

THE CRACK IN THE DOOR

*O*ur story begins—or rather, the discovery that makes it a story took place—in Venice on the morning of 14 January 1662 in the home of an old-clothes dealer. Located in Calle della Stua[1] in the parish of San Cassiano, the dwelling of Bellino Bellini and his family consisted of two rooms: the kitchen and a small bedroom up four wooden steps in a loft. It was a damp, mild Saturday between ten and eleven. While the master of the house was on his rounds collecting old clothes, his wife and their elder daughter went out to shop for groceries in the Panataria,[2] near Rialto. Antonia, the twenty-two-year-old younger daughter, found herself alone with nothing to do. The hour was too early to amuse herself by watching the prostitutes who later on would lean out the windows and doorways on the Fondamenta delle Tette[3] across the canal soliciting clients, an activity encouraged by the authorities to dissuade men from the "sin against nature."[4]

In the tiny apartment next to theirs, divided from the bedroom in the attic by a door bolted on both sides, Antonia could hear the faint sound of a conversation, kept deliberately low, between their new neighbors. From their voices she could tell that they were a man and a woman. Antonia had not seen them arrive, about three weeks earlier, nor had she observed them leaving. Perhaps the man had gone out, but she had no way of distinguishing him from the other men who

---

1. [Calle: Venetian for street; Stua: stove. Place names, except for those with English equivalents such as Venice and Rome, will not be translated either in the text or in the notes unless they are particularly interesting.]

2. [Panataria: bread shop (an alternative name, no longer in use, for Calle delle Beccarie, on which see note 5 below). Many of the streets near Rialto, the largest market zone in Venice, bear names relating to food.]

3. [Fondamenta: street running alongside a canal; Tette: tits.]

4. [Sodomy.]

came in and out of the place. In the first few days they were there, another man had lived with them, and two or three others came up fairly often, including the young proprietor of a paint shop in Calle delle Beccarie[5] in the Panataria. Their harsh, ugly accents made it easy to tell that all of them, including the woman, were from the Bergamo region.[6] In the company of the other men the woman spoke in a normal tone of voice, but now that she was living alone with the one man, she practically whispered. They both acted as if they had to account for everything they said and did to someone who had them under surveillance. Maybe they realized that they were separated from their neighbors only by a thin wooden wall and an old door with a fissure in the middle larger than the other cracks. Young Antonia Bellini, poor and unmarried, God-fearing but lively, a true Venetian in her love of the dramatic and her sense that life was a stage on which she too was a player, decided to satisfy her curiosity.

The crack was not very large. Still, by climbing onto a little bench, Antonia managed to see two figures, both standing. The man, whose back was toward her, was putting a white cloth onto the head of the woman, who appeared to be trying to help him by knotting it under her braids. Then she lit a candle and held it in her right hand. The man in the meantime went over to a trunk painted dark blue, took out a package, and unwrapped it, pulling out a round, shiny object which he placed on the bed, where another white cloth was spread out. The woman knelt, clasped her hands, and raised her face. The man, whose back was still turned, took the shiny box from the bed and opened it. The woman's face, illuminated by the flame of the candle, was clearly visible; she was waiting for something. Then, lo and behold, the man reached out toward her with a communion wafer between his thumb and index finger. The woman received it on her tongue, swallowed it, and bowed her head in prayer. After a few moments, as if awakening from a brief sleep, she blew out the candle and arose.

Her companion bent over to put the package back in the trunk

5. [Beccarie: butcher shops.]

6. [Bergamasques, with their distinctive accent, were the Venetian equivalent of "hillbillies" in the United States. Venetian dramatists often made their lower-class comic characters speak in Bergamasque dialect.]

in the corner. Only then did Antonia notice that he was dressed in black like a priest, although during the strange ceremony he had not worn a surplice and stole. Antonia's first guess, that the woman was ill and in quarantine, proved wrong when she moved quickly after the priest and disappeared with him down the stairs leading to the rooms below. Her black dress, which had wide sleeves like a friar's habit and was cinched at the waist by a leather belt, did not resemble those worn by Venetian commoners or peasant women who came in from the mainland to sell vegetables and chickens. Could she be a nun? She took communion quickly, like someone who was accustomed to doing so as part of her daily routine. But if she were, how could she be living with a priest? Was it legal, Antonia wondered, to administer communion outside a church to an intimate friend who was perfectly healthy?

What Antonia had just seen struck her as too troubling to tell her mother and sister when they returned from the market. She kept it to herself, mulling it over all day and the better part of the night. The more she realized that she was the only one in the house, probably the only person in Venice, who knew about it, the more troubled her conscience became.

Since the next morning was Sunday, Antonia did not need to invent an excuse for going to church. Rather than attending mass in their parish church, San Cassiano, she decided that she needed to make her confession. The confessor of the women in the Bellini family was Don Iseppo Rizzo, a priest in his early forties at the church of San Giovanni Elemosiniere, near the west end of the Rialto.[7] He listened attentively to Antonia's confession without showing the surprise or anger that the young woman had anticipated. He quizzed her on the details, asking her to repeat them, and showed particular interest in the appearance of the two strangers.

7. [San Giovanni Elemosiniere, like all Venetian parish churches in the seventeenth century, was staffed by several priests. Iseppo (Giuseppe) Rizzo, who at this point was third priest, served under the *pievani* (rectors) Antonio Grandi (d. 7 August 1662) and Niccolò Ferro (d. 7 July 1677), after which he himself was named *pievano*. He died on 14 April 1681. Flaminio Corner, *Ecclesiae Venetae antiquis monumentis illustratae,* 18 vols. in 9 (Venice: Giovanni Battista Pasquali, 1749), III, 189.]

Don Iseppo remembered having noticed, a month or so earlier, a middle-aged woman dressed something like a *dimessa*[8] who had taken communion in his church several times without having confessed beforehand. One morning, before saying mass, he had waited near the door into the sacristy until she came in and knelt down in a pew. He was about to go up to her when, from a dark corner of the church, a man of about his own age in a priest's habit approached him in an embarrassed but friendly manner, making a reassuring gesture toward the woman as if to indicate that she was a relative or penitent of his. During communion, it occurred to Don Iseppo that she must be a member of some new order—they were springing up practically every day—because she received the sacrament devoutly, without awkwardness or ostentation. He could not, however, account for the role of the other priest. If the man celebrated mass in some other church, he could have given his protégé communion himself, especially since she apparently did not need to make her confession. Or perhaps the stranger, timid and seemingly bewildered, had nowhere to say mass and was waiting for an invitation. When the mass was over and Rizzo came out of the sacristy, he looked in vain among the pews: the two had left.

The next morning, however, Rizzo gladly welcomed the priest. A man of medium height with dark hair, clean-shaven, he introduced himself by stammering, "Don Pietro, Bergamasque . . ." From the man's looks and behavior, Don Iseppo was able to tell that he was not from the city of Bergamo but rather from its hinterland, possibly a parish in the mountains. He invited the man into the sacristy, indicating with a proprietary air the numerous side altars and the considerable number of worshipers who were responding to his conscientious performance as an urban pastor. The Bergamasque, whose Latin was halting, begged off, giving the impression that he had another engagement, but promised to return the next day. The man and woman never came back to San Giovanni. Rizzo could only conclude that this was just one of those strange encounters so frequent in a city like Venice, where, among people of the most diverse origins and professions,

8. [Dimessa: a woman belonging to an uncloistered order whose members lived in common and engaged in teaching the catechism and various charitable activities. See D.-M. Montagna, "Dimesse della Madonna, Figlie di Maria Immacolata," in *Dizionario degli istituti di perfezione* (Rome: Edizioni Paoline, 1974-   ), III, 505–06.]

there were also defrocked priests still dressed as clerics accompanied by young women who followed some sort of religious rule.

Now that the weight was lifted from her conscience, Antonia went home. As she passed through the Sottoportego delle Carampane,[9] her step quickened, for she was much relieved. The conversation with Don Iseppo had gone much better than she had expected. Because what she had to say was so extraordinary, her confessor had not only overlooked her venial sin of spying on her neighbors—preferable, however, to ogling the fat prostitutes in their low-cut gowns, already at work on Sunday morning—but had even ordered her to go back to the crack in the door and look again, very carefully, since first appearances could be deceiving. Even though Don Iseppo had suggested that she enlist the aid of her mother, she decided to keep the secret to herself for the time being. Now that her mind was clear and firm, she wanted to take another look.

On Monday, 16 January, at the same hour the scene was replayed. Antonia now noticed that the woman's hair was lighter in color than the priest's and that she was shorter and certainly younger than he. Her face, a little too long, made it hard to estimate her age: she might be thirty or even younger, or approaching forty. This time Antonia observed a new and even more disturbing detail of the unusual ceremony. The priest began by spreading a cloth on the woman's bed and lighting a candle as thick as a finger, which he gave her. They knelt down, side by side. With one hand the priest reached toward the woman. Taking hold of a cord tied around her neck and reaching down between her breasts, she helped him pull out a small bag, from which he took the shiny box. He opened it and took out a communion wafer, arose, and without saying a word, administered communion to his companion, bowing and then genuflecting down to the ground. He put the silver container, gilded inside, on the cloth on the bed and went over to a bench to wash his hands in water contained in one of those bowls from Treviso in which apothecaries keep *mostarda*.[10] Then he put the box back into the white bag and placed it in the little sack

9. [Sottoportego: pedestrian passage under a building; Carampane: this corruption of Ca' Rampani became a slang term for prostitutes.]

10. [A fruit conserve, the Italian counterpart of chutney.]

attached to the cord around the woman's neck, which fell back between her breasts.

The strange, solemn rite was obviously a habitual one. Although it had alarmed her at first, the second time Antonia was able to observe it with dispassionate attention. She probably felt, however, that to tell her confessor every detail might prove somewhat embarrassing. It would be better to follow his suggestion and seek the aid of her mother and sister.

From that moment on the women in the Bellini household did nothing but take turns at the crack in the door, even at times when the daily rite was not taking place, so that they would have plenty to tell their father confessor. One day Caterina, the mother, picked up some details that had escaped her daughter which would certainly interest Don Rizzo. As it turned out, however, she had to report them elsewhere than in the confessional, for in the meantime the scrupulous confessor, conscience-stricken himself, had gone to unburden himself in the most appropriate place, the Holy Office of the Inquisition.

The ecclesiastical tribunal, which had been established in its current form in the 1540s to judge cases of obvious or possible heresy, by this time was handling a case load composed primarily of priests who kept concubines, women who cast spells, and artisans and boatmen who had been caught eating meat on fast days.[11] It met in the chapel of San Teodoro, attached to the church of San Marco and reached by passing through the vast sacristy of the basilica.[12] On benches arranged in a horseshoe on the raised semicircular platform sat the papal nuncio, Giacomo Altoviti;[13] the patriarch of Venice, Giovanni Francesco Morosini;[14] and the inquisitor general of the Venetian Republic, the Dominican Fra Ambrogio Fracassini da Brescia, master

11. [On the case load of the Venetian Inquisition in the 1660s, see Anne Jacobson Schutte, "I processi dell'Inquisizione veneziana nel Seicento: La femminilizzazione dell'eresia," in *L'Inquisizione romana in Italia nell'età moderna: Archivi, problemi di metodo e nuove ricerche,* ed. Andrea Del Col and Giovanna Paolin, *Saggi del Ministero per i beni culturali e ambientali* (Rome: Ufficio centrale per i beni archivistici, forthcoming).]

12. [Today one enters the chapel through a courtyard off the west end of the Ponte della Canonica.]

13. [On the Florentine Altoviti (1604–93), nuncio in Venice from 1658 to 1666, see the article by Franco Gaeta in *Dizionario biografico degli Italiani,* II, 576–77.]

14. [Morosini (1604–78) was Patriarch of Venice from 1644 until his death. Antonio Niero, *I Patriarchi di Venezia* (Venice: Studium Cattolico Veneziano, 1961), 127–30.]

of sacred theology.[15] The procurator Pietro Morosini, one of the Three Deputies on Heresy, represented the secular government.[16]

The first thing that the chancellor of the Inquisition, Andrea Vescovi,[17] was required to record—exactly as it was spoken, including dialect forms, gestures, facial expressions, pauses, bursts of tears, and (under torture) exclamations and groans—was the denunciation presented by Father Iseppo Rizzo on 24 January. Two days later the tribunal summoned Caterina Bellini, wife of the used-clothes dealer, age forty-seven. She was still disconcerted by something she had seen just a few hours earlier. This time, in contrast to previous occasions, the priest as well as the woman had taken communion, and he, with his own hands, had pulled the box containing the wafers from between the woman's breasts and put it back. Then, after very carefully washing his hands in the bowl, he had taken a sip of water and given the rest to the woman to drink.

In his capacity as representative of the Church, the inquisitor was naturally obligated to explore the gravest possible consequences of what he had been told. The first matter to be ascertained, therefore, was whether a deliberate act of profanation had occurred. What, he asked, was the attitude of the priest?

Although he was not kneeling, Caterina replied, his head was bowed and he held his folded hands in front of his lips. Then, while the woman was still on her knees, he leaned on his elbows over the bed and, like her, absorbed himself in prayer for the length of time it might take to recite the litanies to the Virgin.[18]

15. [Fracassini (1597–1663) was Inquisitor General of Venice from 30 July 1651 to 5 January 1663, when he was named Bishop of Pola. Venice, Archivio di Stato, Sant'Uffizio, busta 153, Elenco degli inquisitori domenicani; *Hierarchia Catholica medii et recentioris aevi,* IV, ed. Patricius Gauchat, OMConv. (1935; rpt. Padua: Il Messagero di S. Antonio, 1960), 283. As we shall see, the latter stages of this trial were handled by his successor, Agapito Ugoni, also a Dominican from Brescia.]

16. [Pietro di Michiel Morosini (1598–1667), elected Procurator of San Marco in 1657, served two two-year terms (1660–62 and 1664–66) as one of the Tre Savi all'Eresia. Venice, Archivio di Stato, Segretario alle Voci, Elezioni dei Pregadi, registro 18, f. 70v.]

17. [On Vescovi (1622–1714), who was chancellor of the Holy Office for fifty-five years, see Cecilia Ferrazzi, *Autobiografia di una santa mancata,* ed. Anne Jacobson Schutte (Bergamo: Pierluigi Lubrina, 1990), 102, note 103.]

18. [In the early modern era small units of time were almost always expressed in terms of the duration of prayers.]

Was he wearing a surplice and stole?

No, he was dressed in the ordinary black robe of a priest.

Had she noticed anything else? Had she observed them at other times of day?

Signora Bellini blushed—more, no doubt, because of what the inquisitor was implying than because of the necessity to admit that her eyes had been glued to the crack in the door even late at night. But the only other detail she had to report was the priest's putting a bed-warmer between the sheets on the woman's bed.

Then the inquisitor interrogated the discoverer of the strange occurrences. Antonia had nothing new to add. In the twelve days since that first morning, she had peered through the crack at all hours, watching the woman's every move: praying, reading, combing her hair, and of course eating.[19]

On the basis of Rizzo's denunciation and the testimony of the two women, the members of the tribunal determined that they had sufficient evidence to order the arrest of the couple. Shortly after Antonia and Caterina had departed, having sworn to maintain silence about the proceedings, the tribunal decided also to conduct an inspection of the Bellini house in order to see the crack in the door and what could be observed through it. Charged with this job was the chancellor, Vescovi, who thus assumed the dual role of witness and transcriber of his own testimony. The next day they convoked the "valorous" captain of the Holy Office, Michielini, gave him the arrest order, and told him to stand ready to serve it.

The chancellor betook himself to the zone of ill fame, crossed the Ponte delle Tette, passed into Calle della Stua, and stopped at the last house on the fondamenta, which still stands. Its attractive top story with two windows projects over the Rio San Cassiano,[20] which runs on between the buildings toward the Grand Canal.

Opening the door, Donna Caterina immediately recognized Vescovi as the man who during the interrogation had taken down everything she had said, pausing when she hesitated and beginning to write again when she resumed talking. The humble woman would have been

19. [It is worth noting that Antonia—unlike her mother, her older sister, and for that matter Maria Janis—was both able and confident enough to sign her name on the transcript of her testimony. On this issue, see chapter 2, note 6.]

20. [Rio: a minor canal.]

even more embarrassed had she realized that the scribe had reproduced not only her Venetian dialect but also her attempts to express herself in more elegant language: "the woman, having on her head something like a towel with fringes[21] and holding in her hand a lighted[22] candle, I don't know whether it was wax or tallow"; "my daughter Meneghina went to look once, but being impatient and scrupulous,[23] she left without seeing anything." Now he asked her to collaborate. Would she please go to the little room upstairs with the sloping roof, position herself at the crack in the door, and as soon as she saw the two people, run down to tell him?

The lady of the house did just what she was told, and when she called, the chancellor went up the four steps, climbed onto the little bench, and became a privileged spectator. "Having placed my eye at the higher part of the crack in the door, which was made of two pieces,[24] I looked into a little room, which was illuminated by a candle held in the hand of a woman, who at that very moment, on her knees between the windows—or rather window—and a bed, opened her mouth to receive, and then received, a communion wafer."

The agent of the Holy Office stressed the "very great, extraordinary diligence" with which the priest repeatedly inspected his fingers to make sure that not a single fragment of the wafer remained on them. He gave the same close attention to the paten, polishing it several times and bringing the index finger of his right hand to his mouth to lick off the crumbs. Following the purification,[25] the woman was equally attentive to the correct disposition of the elements. Having taken a sip of water, she inspected the bowl, "and with a finger seemed to be pointing at some fragment, whereupon the priest peered into the bowl, felt around with a finger, and brought the vessel to his mouth to empty it."

According to Vescovi, the priest himself put the little silver box back between his companion's breasts, and "having bowed deeply—I

21. *Cai,* Venetian for *frange.*

22. *Impiciata,* an approximation of *appicciata (accesa)*; the alternative prefix struck lower-class people as more elegant.

23. *Impatiente e scrupola:* Latinate, rather technical terms, undoubtedly not the ones Caterina would have used if she had been talking with her peers.

24. [That is, it was an improvised divider between the two apartments, not a normal door made of a single piece of wood.]

25. [Rinsing the mouth with water after communion.]

couldn't tell whether he genuflected—with his hands clasped in front of his mouth, he assumed a devout and contemplative attitude; the woman, who had previously blown out the candle, remained on her knees. So they remained for about the time it takes to say the *Miserere* twice." Once the rite was over, the devout intimacy came to an end. The woman arose and helped the priest to put the objects used during the ceremony into the trunk, after which they went over to the bed and "together turned down the blankets and sheets, one standing on each side of the bed." Then they left, and the little room fell into darkness.

On the following day, Saturday, Captain Michielini made the arrest. If he employed a gondola, he could have tied up right in front of the building, climbing up the two stone steps, slippery with algae, on the curb of the fondamenta. He burst into the apartment of the people from Bergamo, followed by the father commissioner of the Holy Office,[26] the inquisitor's companion,[27] Chancellor Vescovi, and a scribe, who was needed to record the inventory of objects found during the search of the dwelling.[28]

On the priest, apprehended in one of the two little rooms on the lower floor, the captain found a book of prayers to the Virgin and a rosary, as well as a purse containing twenty-five *lire*,[29] which was immediately given back to its owner. The little bag worn around the neck of the woman, who was arrested in her room upstairs, was seized. In the silver box the priests who participated in the arrest found five communion wafers and a sixth which was somewhat misshapen.

The captain left with the two suspects, who were hooded to shield them from recognition and remarks on the part of the whores in the neighborhood, the boatmen on the Grand Canal, and the idlers in front of the Ducal Palace. Then the functionaries who remained in the apartment proceeded to take inventory of its contents, most of

26. [Fra Valentino da Crema.]

27. [The rules of all mendicant orders stipulated that outside the monastery, friars move about in pairs. Fra Ambrogio Fracassini was accompanied everywhere by his designated companion, Fra Francesco Obici, who attested to Michielini's report.]

28. [The *cursor,* Father Antonio Gacci (or Gaggi), also signed the report.]

29. [On this and all other units of currency mentioned, see the Appendix.]

which were stored in the dark blue trunk in the woman's bedroom. There they found books of prayers and other pious works, lives of the saints, formulas of exorcism, the *Revelations of St. Bridget,* letters and other manuscripts, candles, pins, combs, a paper containing grains of incense, and two nun's habits, one white and one black, with long lace-trimmed stoles. Finally, on top of an exposed beam in the ceiling of the same room they discovered three salami, and under Maria's mattress they found two slices of headcheese wrapped in waste paper.

MY NAME IS MARIA JANIS

he suspects were taken to the prison of the Holy Office, located next to the church of San Giovanni in Bragora, a few minutes' walk from Piazza San Marco. Of the two, the priest, because of his ecclesiastical status, was under graver suspicion as primarily responsible for whatever irregular practices—or worse—they had engaged in. On the Monday following their incarceration, however, his companion was interrogated first on the assumption that because, like all women, she was less cultured and weaker, she would further compromise the priest.

The judges saw before them a woman around thirty years old of medium height with an olive complexion, a long face, and medium brown hair. She wore a long black cassock, pulled in at the waist by a leather belt. Rather than being frightened or grief-stricken, she appeared confident, forthcoming, and ready to collaborate. Her submissive and cooperative behavior, however, seemed a bit ostentatious and almost theatrical.

Asked to give "her name, surname, father, mother, brothers, sisters, occupation, and marital status," the woman declared, "My name is Maria Janis, daughter of the late Giovanni Antonio. My mother, who is living, is called Lucrezia. I have a living brother, Giovanni Battista, and two sisters: Caterina, who is single, and my stepsister Isabetta, who is married and lives in Borgo di Vertova. I'm from Colzate di Vertova, and I'm about thirty years old because I was born the year after the plague. My only occupation is to serve God, and since I was unable to enter the convent of Serina Alta, which is not yet finished, I chose to wear this habit of a *dimessa*. I am single."

She was born, then, about twenty kilometers from Bergamo, where the Val Seriana road runs along the river of the same name, in 1632, the year after the plague which devastated Milan. It had struck particularly hard in the Bergamo region in 1631, claiming a number of victims higher than the population listed in the parish registers.[1] With a small stretch of literary imagination, we could consider her a contemporary and even a playmate of Lucia and Renzo Tramaglino's eldest daughter, also named Maria.[2] The protagonist of our story, however, really existed, but she hardly had a childhood. In order to understand how she had turned up in Venice, whose dominion reached west as far as the Bergamasco, we need to take a brief look at the previous stages of her life, examining the information which she herself furnished to the Inquisition.

Maria's family was very poor. At the age of eighteen she felt called upon to consecrate herself to God, but she lacked the means to enter a convent.[3] (The one for needy women under construction in Serina Alta would be completed only after her story came to an end.) She traveled up the Val Seriana to Zorzone, at the foot of a range of mountains whose peaks were often covered with snow even in summer. The curate of Zorzone, Don Pietro Morali, a friend of her father, had achieved a reputation for holiness through his ability to exorcise victims of diabolical possession and perform miraculous cures. Maria put herself under his spiritual direction. For five years she lived outside the village in a hut owned by a man named Colombo. Then she moved closer to the church, into the house of the Palazzi family, who maintained her as a guest in a room in their cellar. One of the Palazzi brothers, called Pietro like the curate, became so fond of her that he too dedicated himself to the religious life and vowed to follow Maria "in life and in death." In the company of this pious bachelor, the young woman could more easily frequent the house of the priest, who lived alone, where she learned how to read the Great Office of the mass, normally reserved to ordained priests and religious.

The bond between the three, which eventually came to resemble an unofficial monastic rule, evoked both respect and puzzle-

1. At Colzate, with a population of 185, 188 deaths were registered; at Vertova, the figures were 838 residents and 1,048 deaths. Lorenzo Ghirardelli, *Storia della peste del 1630,* ed. Mario Testa (Bergamo: Archivio Storico Brembatese, 1974), 357.

2. [The protagonists of Alessandro Manzoni's novel *I promessi sposi* (*The Betrothed*).]

3. [On the economic aspects of entering a convent in the seventeenth century, see Francesca Medioli, *L'"Inferno monacale" di Arcangela Tarabotti* (Turin: Rosenberg & Sellier, 1990), 112–22.]

ment among the villagers. Don Pietro Morali became the target of criticism from the priests nearby because their parishioners were increasingly drawn to Zorzone, where demons were expelled, the lame enabled to walk, the future predicted. The Confraternity of the Holy Belt, which assured indulgences and other benefits to its members, gained more and more adherents.[4] The fame of Zorzone spread so widely through the entire mountainous region that the bishop of Bergamo conducted a cautious investigation. A few months later, when the horizon encircled by the mountains had become too constricting for their aspirations, the three decided to venture further and left the village by night, headed for Rome. They stopped at Botta, the village in the Val Brembana closest to Bergamo, where they were welcomed as guests in the villa of Count Agostino Vitali, the blind nephew of the bishop of Mantua. The count had sought Father Pietro's blessing in a vain attempt to regain his sight. After hosting them generously for two weeks, he departed with them en route to Mantua. There his uncle the bishop refused lodging in the episcopal palace to a vagabond priest followed by a woman and her escort. The three continued their journey on foot, with a mule carrying their baggage, to Loreto, where they paid a pious visit to the Holy House of the Virgin. After twelve more days on the road, they reached Rome.

Internal emigration, especially from rural areas into the cities, was by this time a well-established phenomenon in Italy. During their two-year stay in the papal capital the three pilgrims associated for the most part with landlords, businessmen, and artisans of Bergamasque and Brescian origin. They settled first in Campo dei Fiori in two attic rooms rented from a compatriot, a wholesale dealer in wine, who provided lodging to other immigrants. Then they moved to Piazza Farnese, where their landlord was a canon of San Giovanni in Laterano. Their third home was in Vicolo dei Bresciani, behind the houses of San Pietro. Palazzi, who came from a family of weavers, contributed to their expenses for lodging and food by working as a blanket-maker for a monastery. In the huge, easygoing city of Rome Don Pietro was able to say mass almost anywhere without

4. [See chapter 10, note 1.]

attracting attention or being asked for a dimissory, the letter permitting a priest to exercise his ministry outside the diocese, which his bishop had refused to give him. The rest of the day he spent at home reading his breviary, writing, and praying with Maria. She, after her daily communion, led an even more retired life, following the dictates of the spirit.

Maria made a friend, young Annamaria Casolina, who was poorer than she not only in the economic sense but also because she was married to an unemployed man who probably mistreated her. By giving Annamaria her laundry to wash, Maria helped out as much as she could, and Don Pietro, to keep the woman from an even worse fate, provided a small subsidy which he continued to send her from Venice. It was Casolina who raised the prospect of their moving to another large city, one somewhat less foreign to them because they were its subjects. The two women became so close that both began to receive nightly revelations from on high, which they shared the following morning. Certain of Maria's holiness, the young Roman woman was inspired one night by the Virgin to cut out and sew a special white habit for her friend. From a length of silk purchased by Father Pietro, Annamaria produced a garment with veils, lace, and stoles that was better suited to an altar than to a convent. As Morali later explained, "She did so on the basis of many revelations from the Most Holy Mother of God, who taught her how to make the garment, which Maria was to put on when Her Son called her, and [the Virgin said] that Maria was to go to Venice, for that time would come very soon."

In Venice the three could rely on a small but solidly established colony of Bergamasques, some of whom were relatives. The sausage-maker Giacomo Palazzi, who was Pietro's half brother, arranged lodging for them with a colleague in Santa Margherita, then took them into his own home near the church of the Servites in Cannaregio. During their ten months in Venice the three pilgrims moved twice more, first to a garret at San Mattio di Rialto, the property of the grain merchant Antonio Peverada, and then to the apartment owned by the paint-seller Domenico Calvi in Calle della Stua, where Don Pietro and Maria ended up alone and were arrested.

What, the inquisitor asked, had become of the other Pietro, who had left his father's house and followed them for almost three years?

Maria readily responded: "Pietro is now staying with his brother the sausage-maker at the Servi. He's about forty years old. At home he was a weaver."

The inquisitor now asked why she had gone to Rome with the two men.

"I went to Rome to do the will of God, following the suggestion of Father Pietro Morali and in obedience to him. I subjected myself to him because he represented the person of the Lord. I had made the decision to obey him when I first left home."

Did she have a spiritual father in Rome, the inquisitor inquired, to whom she confessed? And where did she take communion in Rome and here in Venice?

Up to this point in the account of her life, Maria had told a few white lies. She had neglected, for instance, to mention their expulsion from Mantua by the bishop and their stop in Loreto, claiming that from the villa at Botta they had gone directly to Rome without stopping anywhere else, "and our health was so good that in such a long journey we had no problems at all." In matters of faith, however, she could not prevaricate—or she may have believed that the moment had come to reveal her extraordinary spiritual state. Perhaps with greater canniness than candor, she stated that she had never made her confession to anyone in all the time since her departure from Zorzone. There she had confessed to Don Pietro, whom she had continued to "tell what was on her mind" during their stays in Rome and Venice.

In what form and manner had she told what was on her mind?

"When I told Don Pietro what was on my mind, I reported the good inspirations and the temptations I had. I did this standing,[5] and he gave me good advice and reminders, telling me that I must keep my mind always on God. Then he said, 'God bless you in the name of the Father, the Son, and the Holy Spirit. Amen.'"

Although Fra Ambrogio made no direct objection to what

5. [Rather than kneeling, as in the confessional.]

Maria had just said, he reminded her that Christians were obligated to confess at least once a year and to take communion in their own parishes.

Maria, momentarily disconcerted, instinctively shifted the responsibility to her master, in whom she had complete faith. In her response she sounded more like an ordinary working-class woman than a pious aspirant to holiness. "I knew that perfectly well, but because I had subjected myself to the obedience of Don Pietro, I did nothing more. In Rome I took communion in various churches, as I have done here, and in particular I have taken communion about twelve to fifteen times at San Giovanni di Rialto."

Among all the others, Maria chose to specify the little church of San Giovanni Elemosiniere—with its Tintorettos, Pordenones, and Titian's painting of the charitable patron saint, patriarch of Alexandria, over the main altar—whence the denunciation against her had come. Perhaps it was when she realized that she did not really trust Don Iseppo Rizzo that the idea of taking communion at home had begun to appeal to her. Her mention of this church also reminded the inquisitor of her accuser. Therefore he asked her whether she knew or could guess the reason why she had been imprisoned.

"I know why, because when I was arrested, they took from me a silver box, gilded inside, which I kept hung around my neck, in which there were five or six communion wafers. I kept it on me day and night, being very careful not to knock it against anything. And I wore it with great reverence because they were consecrated wafers, with which Don Pietro Morali gave me communion every morning. We did it this way so that I would not have to go around through the streets, and so as not to exasperate people."

By "people," Maria meant priests. Did she fear being admonished for excessive zeal at a time when minutes were measured by the recitation of the Miserere and the implementation of the Counter Reformation was bearing fruit (though not yet as much as its proponents desired)? Certainly not. Instead, what she had said thus far reveals her sense of inferiority, oddly combined with her urgent desire to explain her special situation. Thus, when the inquisitor pointed to the box she had been wearing, which was lying on a table, she arose and went down on her knees. This was the untouchable, indubitable essence of the sacred, recognized as such by the Church, which in contact with her skin consecrated her body, making her breast a tabernacle, her whole person a lodging place of the divine. Without being asked, she was moved to say, "Let me add that this way of giving me communion at home and carrying the consecrated wafers on my body was an inspiration that came to me from God through prayer. When I told Don Pietro about it, he approved and gave me the little box and the wafers."

When had this inspiration come to her?

Two weeks after last Christmas, that is, around Epiphany. From that day on, fifteen or sixteen times, she had received the sacrament at home every morning. Had she been able to, she would have done so on the day of her arrest. We can infer, then, that Antonia had discovered her at her second or third communion, when the sacrament was still being kept in the trunk.

Faced with this almost defiant statement of intent to persevere in such a sacrilegious practice, the inquisitor probably congratulated himself on having decided to interrogate the woman first. What she had said made the priest's position much worse. His next question was whether Don Pietro had also taken communion.

Twice, she replied, he had consumed the large priest's host. Then he had given her the eucharist, using a small wafer from the silver box.

How did the priest conduct this ceremony, and what words did he say during the double communion?

He followed the rite normally performed in church. Together they recited the confession, "and he said 'Domine non sum dignus, Corpus Domini Nostri,' knocking on his breast and making the usual genuflections, and I, kneeling, did the same . . . believing that the Lord was present, as He is in the tabernacles in churches."

The little wafers, called *comunichini,* certainly were not for sale, nor could the priest have asked for them in some sacristy, because he would have had to explain what he intended to do with them outside a church. How, then, had he obtained them, and how had he consecrated them?

He had been given some large hosts for himself, which he brought home in a box and cut with scissors into wafers. They lit two candles, she knelt, and he, dressed in an ordinary priest's cassock, without a missal or any other book, pronounced the words of consecration. "I heard him say the word 'Hoc,' and then in a lower voice he said something else which I didn't quite hear."

With the privilege conferred on him by the sacrament of orders, a priest, by pronouncing the words taught by Christ to the apostles, can consecrate at any time and in any place, even if he is in a state of mortal sin. This Maria had learned during her earliest introduction to Christian doctrine, and the mystery her mind couldn't reach had been reinforced by continual exhortations to faith and obedience. She had believed it. She had accepted and guarded the most holy sacrament in the tabernacle of her breast, taking care not to touch it with her unanointed hands, but preparing herself to receive it daily within her breast from the person ordained to give it to her. Had she erred? The high, learned representatives of the Church would have to decide that. "If I have been deceived, I submit to the judgment of the Holy Office, which I know can separate the true from the false, and in my prayers I always begged the Lord that His will be done."

The interrogation was almost over. Maria believed that she had made a good impression, but she had not yet revealed what was most important to her. She had had an exceptional audience, which had listened to her for four long hours without reproving her or tricking her with overly pointed questions. A few traps laid by Fra Ambrogio she apparently had not recognized; irony was not her strong suit. She arose and again flattered the well-disposed fathers, coming close to thanking them in a sort of improvised leave-taking: "Let me add that I find myself much consoled by being before this Holy Office, as I was at the time of my arrest, since I am sure that the Lord God will see me through."

Her attention was called to the objects seized from the little apartment in Calle della Stua, which were lined up on a table. They seemed like the remains of an austere but free life, full of the most varied expectations and unknown possibilities. She almost caressed them with her gaze. "These are my clothes. I had the white robe made for me in Rome, with the stoles to tie around me to make myself worthy at the end of the road I had to travel. The black robe I had made in Venice, along with the other things, except the books and other writings of the priest, including his certificates and attestations, which must be preserved. The Trevisan bowl is the one used for the ablution." Then she saw the three salami, artfully placed at the end of the row. Maria looked at them unperturbed, saying without hesitation, "Those are his, too."

She signed the transcript by drawing a large, firm cross,[6] just like the large, ceremonious sign of the cross made by a parish priest during rogations as he blesses fields at the intersection of two roads.

6. [That Maria could read but not write, as she stated explicitly during her first interrogation, was by no means unusual in this period. In Europe until the nineteenth century, the teaching of writing was separate from and subsequent to the teaching of reading. People in the lower classes, if they were educated at all, often achieved only the first stage of literacy. See François Furet and Jacques Ozouf, *Reading and Writing: Literacy in France from Calvin to Jules Ferry* (Cambridge: Cambridge University Press, and Paris: Editions de la Maison des Sciences de l'Homme, 1982), especially 166–91; and Ferrazzi, *Autobiografia* (full citation in chapter 1, note 17), 103–6.]

THE HEAVENLY SUPPER

*T*he next day, 31 January, Don Pietro Morali was conducted from the prison to the chapel of San Teodoro for his first hearing. The chancellor's introductory notes describe him as around forty years old, of ordinary height and thus somewhat taller than his pupil. His hair, cropped short, was darker than hers, and since he was clean-shaven, it was clearly apparent that his complexion also tended toward olive. On the left side of his forehead was the furrow of a scar. He was dressed like a priest from the country, where changes in fashion arrive late even for ecclesiastics: his cassock touched the ground.

He was a native of Zambla, eight kilometers west of Oltre il Colle at the highest point of the circular range of foothills below the mountains that rise up more than two thousand meters. As a boy tending the grazing cows, he could have seen down to his left the village of Zorzone, huddled around the little church with the square bell tower, which he would later serve as curate for twelve years. The road from Oltre il Colle, which climbs up the Val Brembana in hairpin turns, descends after Zambla into the Val Seriana, skirting Colzate and Vertova, Maria's towns, and down into the plain of Bergamo. This was the route Pietro usually followed to pursue his studies in Crema, Lodi, and Cremona, where he was ordained respectively subdeacon, deacon, and priest, after which he studied theology in Milan. But sometimes he would have taken the more convenient mule track heading south from Oltre il Colle to Nembro via Serina, which at midpoint passed through Trafficanti, a name alluding to the flow of Venetian goods directed toward Switzerland and Germany along this route in order to avoid Spanish customs dues in the Duchy of Milan.

His account of the voyage and stays in Rome and Venice accorded with that furnished by his disciple. He also volunteered that they had not been welcomed by the bishop of Mantua and provided additional details about their life in the two cities, which demonstrate that he had obviously had closer contacts with Bergamasque circles, particularly in Venice, where he had bought the silver box in a compatriot's shop at Rialto.

The inquisitor was naturally curious to know why they had moved house so frequently in Venice.

They had done so, Morali replied, in order not to trouble their kind compatriots, who had not only put them up without charging rent but had also paid for his and Pietro Palazzi's meals.

But weren't there three of them at first, before Palazzi moved out? Who provided the woman's meals?

Don Morali was happy to explain. "The woman was content with her privilege."

The inquisitor clearly didn't understand. What privilege? He ordered Morali to explain himself.

"The privilege was to live on communion alone."

Fra Ambrogio turned toward the two prelates, whose expressions showed him that they were just as taken aback and perplexed as he. Interrogating the defendant, however, was his responsibility, and he had at his disposition many manuals (the most venerable of which was the *Malleus maleficarum,* first published in Strasbourg around 1486) on how to conduct the trial of persons who had departed from the true faith and therefore fallen into heresy. He asked that the accused "state more plainly in full detail what this privilege was and how it was practiced."

Don Pietro had to exercise all the self-control at his command in order to take full advantage of an opportunity he had long awaited, which now presented itself in especially favorable circumstances. "The privilege," he replied, "was that having taken communion, she needed no other food until communion the next day."

Was this some sort of play on words? What did he mean by "no other food"? Certainly a person could fast for a day. Or did the woman take communion more than once a day? "How much time passed between one communion and the next?"

Apparently feeling that he had the situation under control, the priest responded confidently, lucidly, and logically: "The time that passed was from one morning to the next."

The Dominican began to have an inkling of what Morali meant, but the consequences of the defendant's statement seemed wildly improbable. Thinking aloud, the inquisitor wondered whether, if the woman took communion every morning, the accused intended to suggest that every day she went without food.

Morali confirmed the speculation: every morning she took communion and then went without food all day and all night.

Repressing his incredulity, Fra Ambrogio sought to skirt the obstacle of an obvious impossibility. He had regained enough control of himself to be able to phrase the next question precisely: "Since when has Maria taken communion every day, and where?"

Father Pietro responded directly. Since Palm Sunday of 1657 (almost five years before she was arrested), Maria Janis had taken communion every morning: in Rome in various churches, and here in Venice in the monastic churches of the Servites (Santa Maria de'Servi), the Theatines (San Nicola da Tolentino), the Discalced Carmelites (Santa Maria del Carmine), the Conventual Dominicans (Santi Giovanni e Paolo), the Observant Franciscans (San Francesco della Vigna), the Reformed Franciscans (San Bonaventura), and the Carmelite nuns (Santa Teresa), as well as in the parish churches of San Geremia and San Giovanni di Rialto.

And had he himself ever taken communion?

Put almost automatically, the question seemed unimportant. The rite in the attic—which until a few minutes ago had seemed to be the only serious charge, and about which the tribunal was informed in every detail—was on the point of being reduced to a mere accessory fact, though Morali, the prime suspect, had not yet spoken of it. The tribunal had to listen once again to the story of the little bags, the box containing the communion wafers, and the Trevisan bowl. On all these matters Don Pietro, not realizing that his judges had already heard about them, supplied the minute particulars, as if he thought that his detailed explanation would reinforce his innocence. His account was characterized by genuine naiveté, particularly from the erotic, sexual point of view. It was he, he explained, who took "from the neck and breast of the woman the box contained in those little bags." He obviously thought that it would be worse to let them think that the woman had touched the pyx with her unanointed hands than to admit that he had put his consecrated hands between her breasts. What he said, however, gives us a clearer idea of how they had come upon the idea of her feeding at home on the bread that, according to the Gospels, satisfies all human hunger.

In order to survive physically, Maria had to take communion every morning. On difficult days, when she realized that she would trouble some parish priest by asking him to open the tabernacle for her alone, the holy sacrament appeared to her in the form in which it was shown to the people. In her vision, the large host with which the celebrant communicated was at the center of the ostensory, surrounded by darts and rays of golden light: the breath of God condensed in a mist, the heart of the Church and the fruits of the earth in the process of fusing in the miracle of transubstantiation. At the church of San Giovanni the woman from Vertova must have sensed that the priest Don Iseppo was suspicious, and after he pressed her escort to say mass there, she realized that the door of that church, too, was about to be slammed in their face. Then she had another, more complex vision the meaning of which was transparent: the Virgin appeared to her, holding the sacrament in her hand. Maria interpreted this not only as a concession but as an explicit suggestion. The vision meant that Don Pietro could consecrate the host by saying only the key words of the formula: *Hoc est enim corpus meum.*

At first her master was reluctant to do so. In exercising his ministry up to this time, he had cut some corners, but he had always consecrated the host during the celebration of the mass. Therefore he declined. Like any woman sure of obtaining what she wants most from the man she loves, Maria did not insist. Instead they prayed together and in the morning shared the thoughts they had had and their good intentions for the coming day. The good priest began to reconsider. Was he not in the company of a saint who had received from heaven the privilege of living without touching food? Didn't she have the right to what she was asking? And hadn't this been guaranteed by the gesture of the Virgin, who intended to continue employing Maria in her service? After five years of living a life of perfection, was it likely that Maria had descended to cheating?

The next morning Father Morali went out to obtain some hosts, returned, and cut them with scissors into wafers. As he was about to consecrate them, however, his doubts returned. Having just finished saying her morning prayers, his pupil ended her meditation and, rising to her feet, exhorted him "not to worry, because during her prayers it had been revealed to her in her heart that her celestial meal had been prepared." Perhaps the natural wish not to disappoint such a confident expectation was the deciding factor in his going ahead to consecrate the wafers and give her communion.

Some days later, to test the man again and at the same time convince him that she had not tricked him, she told him that she had had to wage battles with the Devil, who was trying to persuade her that what she was taking was not the real sacrament because the priest had not celebrated mass. To keep her from insisting that he also say mass in the apartment, he probably assured her that these were only diabolical temptations. She let the matter drop rather than run the risk of seeming like a child who is never satisfied.

Again seeking to discern the truth through prayer, they became convinced that the short formula was sufficient to consecrate the bread. They were reassured also by the spiritual and physical state of the beneficiary. Maria affirmed that she felt the same effect as when she took communion in church, and she was neither hungry nor thirsty.

From that point on she had no further doubts. True, she had two diabolical temptations after she began to keep the sacrament under her clothes, a decision she reached by a process of logical deduction. It was not respectful, and probably illegal, to store it along with miscellaneous possessions in the dark blue chest or give it to the priest, who had to pass through the streets, where he could not help encountering prostitutes. She, on the contrary, never left her room, and on her breast the angels' bread could rest undisturbed, radiating throughout her body. Then, however, she was accosted by a man dressed as a king with a crown on his head who told her that he, not what she guarded at her breast, was the real Lord. On another occasion she saw, glimmering before her eyes, a big, beautiful host, perfectly formed but with a hole in the middle like a coin of small denomination. (As the old saying goes, "It isn't worth a plugged nickel.")

It is difficult to tell whether in reporting these visions, the woman was trying to obtain something that surpassed the privilege of carrying the body of Christ on her own body. In addition to being an aspiring saint, however, she was also a woman disposed to recognize that she could be mistaken—just like her master, who did not hesitate to reveal his doubts and perplexities to the judges of the Holy Office.

At the end of Morali's long account, the inquisitor showed that he had not entirely recovered from the shock produced by the revelation about Maria's total fast. As if he were giving his fellow priest one more chance, he asked him whether "it was really the case that Donna Maria, taking communion, was never hungry nor thirsty and never ate and drank."

Don Pietro willingly reiterated what he had said. "Certainly she has never eaten nor drunk from the time I told you until now, although I have heard that because at present, in prison, she does not have her celestial meal, she is eating."

And she didn't eat before? How could he be so sure?

Because he had tested her. As he was preparing for the pastoral visit of the bishop of Bergamo, he had decided to make absolutely certain that he could lay before the prelate a truly extraordinary matter. One morning, therefore, he took great care to ensure that Maria did not receive communion and had nothing to eat during that day and the following night. After twenty-four hours she was so weak that she could hardly make her way to the church. She dragged herself there "little by little, as if she were half-dead, but after taking communion, she revived and regained her strength, and from then on I have never doubted, nor do I doubt now, that she has this gift from heaven."

Did he reveal all this to Bishop Barbarigo? And if so, what was his reaction?

"I told him that this young woman lived on communion alone through a special privilege, whereupon he and a Jesuit priest who was with him examined the young woman and were satisfied. Monsignor Bishop said, 'This must be true,'[1] and all this was taken down in the transcript of the visit."

That, however, is not exactly how it happened. As we shall see later, Father Morali's version of the episcopal visitation was either ingenuous or deliberately misleading. At this point the interrogation, which had lasted three hours, was almost finished. The friar showed him the portable pyx, which the priest recognized as his. Two lamps were lit, enabling Don Pietro to take a close look inside. When he saw

1. ["Bisogna che questa cosa sia vera": an ambiguous subjunctive construction, rendered here, as Morali probably intended it to be understood, in the least dubious of several possible forms. See also chapter 13, note 2.]

that the hosts were those he had cut with scissors and then consecrated, he fell on his knees, just as Maria had done. If we were outside
the scope of dogma in the realm of everyday life, where people so
often put on an act to impress others and thus achieve their objectives, we might be tempted to define his behavior as an act of self-
aggrandizement.

The inquisitor was not so skeptical or free and easy. Once the
priest had been taken back to prison, Fracassini put on his surplice
and stole, had two torches lit, and went to his monastery, San Domenico, to put the little box containing the bags sewn by Maria into the
tabernacle of the church. Early the next morning, in the presence of
the commissioner and chancellor of the Holy Office and his companion, he celebrated mass. During communion he pulled the package
out of the ciborium, opened it, and reverently consumed the five and
a half wafers. Thus the most authoritative and fear-inspiring representative of Catholic orthodoxy in the Venetian Republic, whom bishops and cardinals bowed to and called "my father," took communion
with bread consecrated by a heretical or merely ignorant priest whom
not even the jailers respected. An exponent of another kind of hier-
archy or a different ideology might at the very least have shared the
hosts with his associates. But the inquisitor's action exemplifies the
power of the seventeenth-century Church and thereby contains in a
nutshell the central point of our story.

SALAMI AND THE
COUNTER REFORMATION

*W*hile interrogating the defendants, the Inquisition was simultaneously pursuing two other avenues of investigation. It had made contact with the inquisitor of Bergamo and had ordered the priest of San Giovanni Elemosiniere to talk again with Caterina Bellini and her daughters about the so-called fast of the woman under arrest, since at the end of her interrogation Antonia had stated that she had seen the woman eat.

The first response came from Bergamo. Fra Vincenzo Maria Rivali da Bologna, the inquisitor, reported that the bishop's representative had "heard with particular pleasure about the incarceration of that Pelagino priest and his female disciple."[1] Fra Vincenzo had already charged the vicar of the Val Seriana district with gathering information on the spot. For the time being he could only state that until 1659 Father Pietro Morali had been in Zorzone, "where he was held to be a saint who performed miracles and was in spiritual charge of that Maria da Vertova, whose holiness he publicized." There had been such a great influx of the faithful into Zorzone that, in his capacity as inquisitor, Fra Vincenzo had wanted to open an investigation, but he had been restrained from doing so by someone in the episcopal curia. He had managed, however, to see that during the visit of the new bishop, Gregorio Barbarigo, to Zorzone, inquiries had been made in the hope of quashing the rumors spreading among the people and, if possible, getting "that miserable priest and the woman as well into the hands of

1. [Rivali automatically assumed that Morali was among the followers of Giovanni Filippo Casola of Milan, who had been under investigation in the diocese of Bergamo, above all in the Val Camonica, since the middle of the previous decade. These mystics, who emphasized mental prayer and whose antinomian approach (at least in the opinion of the Holy Office) encouraged sexual license, were called Pelagini after Casola's Milanese headquarters, the Oratory of Santa Pelagia. See Gianvittorio Signorotto, *Inquisitori e mistici nel Seicento italiano: L'eresia di Santa Pelagia* (Bologna: Il Mulino, 1989), especially 242–44.]

the Holy Office." Having laid hands on two documents relating to that pastoral visit, he sent them on to Venice. And he promised to forward as soon as possible the transcripts of the interrogation of witnesses in the area, "so that hypocrite and his woman can be punished."

As far as countryfolk were concerned, any relationship between a man and a woman had to end up in bed. Nevertheless, when such a thing actually happened, they were surprised and horrified. For Fra Ambrogio, who supervised the operation of Inquisition tribunals throughout the Venetian state and dealt firsthand with misbehavior in the labyrinth of Venice itself, sexual incontinence on the part of priests and religious was an everyday occurrence. On the other hand, he had rarely encountered devotion and rigor carried to excess in every sense of the word. As we have just seen, he was a man of faith, and perhaps he found for the first time a need to bridle rather than spur on faith. In the letter and documents sent him by his colleague and subordinate in Bergamo, which reached him two days later by special messenger, the case appeared in a new, comparatively mundane light. But to the inquisitor in Venice, things were not as clear and simple as they seemed in Bergamo. The women of the Bellini family had been peering through the crack to observe something other than sex, and Caterina at least was not reluctant to tell everything she had seen.

After having been given a week to think things over, Don Pietro Morali appeared for the second time before the tribunal. The first question put to him was the usual one: whether he had anything to add to what he had previously said.

The priest from the mountains, with the burning eyes that might indicate that he was inspired or insane, again took the oath to tell the truth, the whole truth, and nothing but the truth. He appeared determined either to challenge the inquisitor or to take refuge in what he had already said. He had nothing else to say, he stated, except that he had no doubts about the "privilege given by Our Lord God to his daughter Maria to live on communion alone."

Fra Ambrogio decided that if this was a case of pretense pure and simple, there the stiff-necked embodiment of it was, right in front of him in the chapel of San Teodoro, clearly being maneuvered by the Evil One. There was no need, then, to wait for the results of other investigations in progress; he had to take the Devil by the horns here and now. Demonstrating his suspicion of everything Morali said, he began to implement this strategy. From whom, he asked, had the priest learned that the woman was eating in prison?

It had been easy to figure out. In the first place, he had seen that a daily half-kilo of bread, called the bread of San Marco, and an occasional bowl of soup were provided by the Confraternity of San Bartolomeo to all prisoners certified to be poor. Since those who had to pay for their food contested the free distribution to the others, a person could hardly refuse these rations.[2] Besides, the woman was no longer receiving her heavenly supper. (Nor, we can add, could she have been receiving it for the simple reason that, having been charged with sacrilege, she was in a state of mortal sin.)

Before she was imprisoned—the friar insisted on this point so that the chancellor could write down the response in black and white—on the days she took communion, that is, every day, he had never seen her eat or drink, neither during the day nor at night?

Never: he had never seen her eat or drink, neither during the day or at night.

Had he heard others say, or had she herself told him, that she had taken food?

No one whatsoever, and particularly not she, had ever told him that she had eaten. In fact, at the very beginning, when he found it difficult to believe, he had had Pietro Palazzi stick close to her in order to watch her and report on whether she ate.

Was there any possibility that without his knowledge, someone could have been giving her food which she consumed on the sly?

"Having been very careful about this matter, I must say no."

Before exhibiting proof to the contrary, the inquisitor renewed his invitation to tell the truth, which amounted to a warning.

The defendant replied that he had no doubt about anything he had said.

Then the physical evidence was produced. During the search of the woman's room, "under the mattress near the head of the bed, two slices of headcheese were found, and hidden on top of a roof beam there were two and a half whole salami, and in the chest in the kitchen

2. For further information about conditions in Venetian prisons, see Giovanni Scarabello, *Carceri e carcerati a Venezia nell'età moderna* (Rome: Istituto della Enciclopedia Italiana, 1979).

below a good deal of bread." The salami were now lying on the table. The defendant was invited to come forward and inspect them. Did he recognize them?

He recognized the salami as his property. Pietro Palazzi had brought them from his brother's shop, and he had put them on the beam, just as he had hidden the slices under the straw mattress.

Why had he hidden these provisions?

So that people who came to the house would not find them and he could have something to eat when he got hungry.

Morali's explanation was rather feeble. At this point it seems to us that the house of cards is about to collapse, and that such a pathetic lie need not concern us further. The inquisitor showed signs of impatience. For Maria, headcheese, already sliced, was right at hand, and she could have got at the bread in the cupboard whenever she went downstairs. Why not admit it?

Don Pietro retorted that yes, it might appear that Maria could have eaten the bread and headcheese without his noticing. But that could not have happened, because he would have known about it.

How? Would the witness please explain himself?

At this point, instead of looking for a way out, one could say that the defendant did everything to compromise both of them and their entire past. He replied that since the woman had always remained faithful and obedient to him, she never did anything without asking his opinion first. She was not at peace with her conscience unless she told him everything.

The inquisitor then shifted to explicit threats. The witness must tell the truth about whether the woman ate and drank, or else the Holy Office would employ upon him "the appropriate measures, legal and physical, in order to get it."

"I have already told the truth as I have known and know it."

Though his defense was full of holes, the priest's good faith could not be shaken. The only recourse for his fellow ecclesiastic on the other side of the bench was to return to other charges, some probable, others already established. There was no need to strain himself. As before, the defendant was almost encouraged to cooperate with these lines of questioning, on which he could perhaps reinforce his position. Asked where he had celebrated mass after his departure from Zorzone, he enumerated all the churches and chapels along his route, ending at the Frari,[3] where he had been denied permission to celebrate because he lacked a dimissory.

For all that time, then, he had celebrated mass without authorization from his bishop?

Directly and through intermediaries, he had asked Monsignor Barbarigo to grant him the dimissory. The bishop had said he would do so but then failed to live up to his promise. Therefore Morali had used the dimissory given him when he had gone to study in Milan.

Were the letters, affidavits, and manuscripts seized in Calle della Stua all his?

All of them, except for a little book in which Pietro Palazzi had kept a diary of their voyage.

Hadn't he too kept a sort of diary?

Not really. From the time he left Zorzone until the day of his arrest he had been working, among other things, on writing the life of Maria. (No saint, and probably only some completely different type of woman, could have succeeded in transforming both her escorts into biographers.)

While he was curate in Zorzone, did Maria come to visit him in his house?

She came to perform spiritual exercises.

Did she confess to him?

She confessed to no one else.

In Rome and here in Venice, did she confess to another priest?

She had no need to. She confided in him and he "removed her scruples, having found nothing in her requiring absolution."

In Zorzone, did she come to see him about other matters?

She came not to consult him about practical matters, but only so that he could guide her in her spiritual life.

Why had he decided to abandon his pastorate and depart with her?

They had both been inspired to do so by the Holy Spirit so as to avoid the villagers' curiosity and so that she could continue to take her celestial sustenance.

It was a vicious circle. The inquisitor by himself could not break

3. [Santa Maria Gloriosa de'Frari, the Conventual Franciscan church in Venice.]

it, especially since by now he probably realized that there was no devil to take by the horns. Nothing remained but to draw on the report transmitted by his colleague in Bergamo and use it to reprove and threaten the defendant. Hence his reaction was all the sharper. "This is a subterfuge and an invention because Monsignor Bishop had ordered you to send away Maria da Vertova, and that was the only way to do the will of God rather than follow your own inclination."

Don Morali cowered. He had ordered Maria to go back to her family, but she had replied that she was inspired to follow him, especially since her living on communion alone was a secret.

This, too, was a subterfuge. Everyone in Zorzone knew about it!

This time Don Pietro was able to gain a point. In Vertova, where he had been told to send her, no one knew about it.

Misled by the mountain priest's ingenuousness, Fra Ambrogio had undervalued his natural astuteness, which emerged whenever he felt that he was being provoked. From the dossier spread out before the inquisitor, it appeared that his colleague in Bergamo had intended to bring charges or at least wanted to interrogate the suspect priest.

The defendant confirmed that impression. After the bishop's visit, the father inquisitor had called him to Bergamo to ask him whether there really was a woman under his care who did not eat. Father Pietro had responded that there was. The friar replied that if that were true, it would be a great thing, but that he did not believe it. It was true, the curate had told him, and could be established by conducting a test.

The same Gordian knot, the same maze: Fra Ambrogio was tired. He rose and approached the table on which the physical evidence was laid out. Did the defendant recognize Maria's white habit? Where and for what reason had it been made?

To us Morali's response may sound somewhat mocking, but in fact it was not. Genuinely convinced that at long last the moment had come to reveal everything, he replied, "This is a great interrogation, and I must tell the truth." He went into detail about the special garment sewn in Rome by Annamaria Casolina following inspiration by the Virgin, who ordered that when her Divine Son called Maria, she put it on.

What did all this mean?

Morali had understood it as follows. Our Lord God wanted to

make Maria's incredible privilege known to the whole world, and the moment had come to do so, "since at the present time within Christendom, faith in the most holy sacrament is weak or lacking."[4]

At this point, even though Father Pietro had not yet confessed to the inquisitor, his motivation becomes clear enough to us. He and his Maria represent the harvest of the Counter Reformation, a more abundant one than even the popes, the fathers of the Council of Trent, and the Jesuits had expected. According to the exponents of Catholic renewal, it was not sufficient for people to throw themselves at the feet of the crucified Christ and weep on command over misdeeds they had never in fact committed. Instead, they must recover their enthusiasm, reinforce their zeal, embrace the mysteries of the faith without inquiring into them, infect each other with divine love. Only thus could the Church replenish the ranks of the army of the faithful, kept on alert by fear of damnation. Such a "spiritual plane" would inspire, consciously or unconsciously, the totalitarian ideologies of the future. But Pietro Morali and Maria Janis had gone even further. Spontaneous fermentation, not the injection of authorized yeast, was making their faith overflow. For this reason they posed problems to the inquisitor.

4. In the Protestant sphere, which before the ferocious repression in the Valtellina (1620) had extended almost as far south as the Bergamo region, the doctrine of transubstantiation was denied.

5

THE THIRD MAN

*P*ietro Palazzi, whose name has turned up frequently in this account, had abandoned his father's house and his occupation in order to follow the priest and the woman everywhere they went. He had been charged by Morali with keeping an eye on Maria, who had utilized him to lend respectability to her frequent visits to the rectory. Was he the same sort of person as his associates? It would seem so when one leafs through the barely legible *Memorial of Our Departure,* a series of disconnected exhortations strung together as if the writer had never found an organizing principle, which is often the case when an uneducated person puts pen to paper. Toward the end, the priest and the woman had been thinking about sending him on his way. For the celestial supper to be consumed at home, even their faithful and useful escort would have been one too many. Once his half brother the sausage-maker had called him away to work in his shop, the idea of the domestic communion *à deux* could gradually emerge, just as a man and woman alone together in a cold room tend to huddle closer and closer together.

From Maria's spontaneous admission, the inquisitor had formed an image of Palazzi as a man in love who had resigned himself to the impossibility of winning her hand. According to her, "During the time I lived in his father's house he became very fond of me. His affection kept growing from the first moment he laid eyes on me in Zorzone. Therefore he wanted to be by my side in life and in death; he told me that he wanted to share my fate."

The eldest of the three, Palazzi was only a year older than Morali, who called him "that young man," and he kept himself in the background. Although he referred to Maria in secular terms as a "marriageable young woman," he was persuaded and respectful of the others' holiness. In matters concerning the soul, therefore, he assumed the role of servant, companion, and disciple.

Fracassini asked whether he had sought instruction in spiritual matters from the woman or the priest.

First from the priest, Palazzi replied, because he knew how to distinguish good from evil, and then from the woman in order to receive good advice from her.

Why had he decided to leave his village and go away with them? Had he been recruited or persuaded by someone? When and how did they depart?

Pietro Palazzi, a weaver by trade, replied that he had joined the curate and Maria of his own free will, recognizing that they were fine people in every respect and having decided with them to depart together. They left on a night in February 1659 with a mule loaded with their belongings. The three of them were on foot.

Why did they leave at night?

"To avoid the crowds and the uproar."

What kind of uproar did they fear during the day that led them to decide to leave at night?

During the day the village would have been filled with people flocking to Zorzone from all over to witness the departure of Father Pietro and Maria, who were held to be holy people.

On what grounds were the two considered to be holy?

Palazzi offers us two complementary models of perfect Counter Reformation Catholic comportment: Morali the good pastor and Janis the ideal layperson. The former, based almost exclusively on countering the Protestant challenge, is focused on externals; the latter involves passive obedience. "Father Pietro taught good doctrine in conformity with the divine precepts and Christian Doctrine,[1] advocating in particular humility, the exercise of sincere prayer to God, and frequent communion." As for Maria, "her good advice was to observe the commandments of God and the Church, to deny one's will, to mortify one's body, to suffer—even to welcome—injuries, and to do other good works."

Following such precepts assiduously, however, did not automatically convey holiness, which descended from heaven upon the most

1. [This term is capitalized because it is the official name of the catechetical effort mounted after the Council of Trent by such proponents of the Counter Reformation as the future saint Carlo Borromeo, Cardinal Archbishop of Milan (1538–84), and expanded in the seventeenth century.]

faithful (and fortunate) as the greatest of privileges. Thus Don Pietro exorcised the possessed by making the sign of the cross and invoking the names of Jesus and Mary. The priest's disciple Maria, who lived on communion alone but kept it a secret, had become for Palazzi, an observant Christian not touched by special grace, an intercessor with God and the Virgin for the remission of his sins.

The inquisitor's frame of reference did not, of course, permit him to speculate, as we are inclined to do, about the sense of complete inferiority that gave rise to such an attitude, nor about how it could unleash an aspiration of a similarly absolute character to total, exceptional freedom from punishment. Fra Ambrogio da Brescia, however, was no fool, and besides, he was determined to get at the facts. Hence he asked the witness, if the woman did not manifest her privilege, how did he know about it?

Don Pietro told him when he asked Palazzi's father and brother to lodge Maria in their house.

How long had Maria stayed with them? Had he ever seen her eat?

She was with them two years, and neither he nor anyone else in the house had seen her eat. During the trip, the stops, and the periods of residence in Rome and Venice she had continued to fast. She said that she did not get hungry, nor did she even know what hunger was.

At this point the inquisitor began to realize that lined up against him were not two but rather three allies, in complete agreement and equally inflexible, the third of whom, at liberty though under oath, was risking prison despite the fact that he did not pretend to exceptional holiness. To make sure that such was the case, and perhaps also to offer Palazzi a way out, he asked him in an unofficial, friendly manner whether he had really "never, never" seen her eat during all that time, and whether he believed that her claim was true.

The weaver followed the verbal lead, at the cost of letting himself become inextricably entangled in the case. "Never, never in all this time have I seen her eat, and I believe it because I have seen it with my own eyes."

Aware that he had scored, the Dominican resumed his detached, neutral tone of voice. Before pressing his advantage, he put to the witness some trivial questions designed to catch him in contradictions. How long had it taken them to get from Botta to Rome?

Traveling partly on foot and partly on horseback, about twenty days.

What trade did he follow in Rome?

He wove blankets in the shop of one Sasso, a Genovese, then for Agostino, also Genovese, and for the Augustinian monks, "earning from three to four *paoli* a day, and sometimes nothing because there was no opportunity to work."

Did Maria take communion every morning?

Every morning, both during the journey and in Rome and Venice.

The inquisitor feigned an outburst aimed at intimidating the witness: he had lied and should keep in mind that he was under oath. It just wasn't possible that in only twenty days they could have completed a journey that long, given the fact that the woman had to take communion every morning. And since he was employed weaving blankets in Rome, how could he know whether she really took communion daily and refrained from eating?

Pietro Palazzi maintained that he had told the truth. During the trip, when they arrived at a stopping point in the evening, the first thing they did was to find the church and make arrangements with the priest for mass next morning. As for her taking communion in Rome, he assumed that she did so because one Good Friday when the sacrament was not distributed, "she was all dejected and fainted."

The father accuser moved on to the "little book" in manuscript bearing the modest but at the same time presumptuous title *Memorial of Our Departure,* in which he had underlined various passages.

Yes, Palazzi replied, he had written it for his own satisfaction.

Among the rapturous phrases, one that frequently recurred, "the gift of faith," had immediately raised suspicion in the mind of the master of sacred theology. It might in fact be a personal, updated interpretation of the Protestant principle of justification by faith alone without works (or in other words, to be saved, it is sufficient to believe), condemned by the Council of Trent in one of its earliest sessions. From whom had the witness received the gift of faith so often referred to in the little book?

It had never crossed Palazzi's mind that the central concepts of the Reformation, which had made their way over the Alps and taken root nearby in the Valtellina, might have come to Zorzone and cohab-

ited in the hearts of simple people with the most submissive orthodoxy. He replied without hesitation, "I believe that I have received this
gift of faith from God, as it says in the Gospel, and I believe according
to the Gospel in one God, nor do I doubt any part of the holy faith."

Fra Ambrogio pitilessly cited a passage from the weaver's book
and asked him to confirm it. "Do you have faith, then, that you can
work and do everything to the honor of the Lord, and that you have
the keys of the heavenly treasury and can take what you want
from it?"

The pious artisan had never dared to hope that he might find
such a highly placed reader. Blushing, he found the strength to follow
the inquisitor's lead in the hope of clarifying and even improving on
what he had written. "I am confident and certain that I can do everything to the honor of the Lord, and that I have the keys of heaven that
enable me to take anything whatever which is to the honor and glory
of God."

"Are you certain and confident that you have been miraculously
saved from the world and from Hell?"

"I am also confident that I have been saved from the world and
from Hell because my parents wanted to find me a wife and did not
want me to leave home, and because I have been freed from the doubts
that troubled me. And [I am confident that] I can do the penance
imposed on me by confessors and need not suffer further punishment."

"Are you certain and confident of being able to obtain from the
Lord God whatever you want from Him?"

"Not worldly things, however."

"Do you have faith that the sacrifice of your prayer is dearer to
God than what one can do in Rome?"

What the diarist feared was being suspected of pride and a sort
of insubordination, not of sympathy with Protestantism, more corro-
sive and therefore more greatly feared and persecuted. He drew this
inference from the expression on the friar's face, as well as from the
peculiar weight assigned to his words, read in a suspicious, malevolent
tone in the presence of the two silent but attentive prelates. Therefore
he interrupted the flow of questions and answers in order to make
clear that he did not recall why he had used the word "Rome." It had
certainly not been his intent to cast doubt "on the good done by
members of religious orders and friends of God."

A psychoanalyst might interpret Palazzi's choice of words by suggesting that at the time he wrote them, he was fed up with Rome, where he had to spend whole days separated from Maria, and that he dreamed of their returning to his own house in Zorzone to pray together. The Dominican, too, had no doubt about the sentiment that linked the layman with Maria, but in his role of inquisitor, he needed to probe further into Pietro's no doubt excessive sublimation. For this reason he made him recite the names and titles which he used in the little book to refer to Maria.

Palazzi cited them from memory. "I called her Maria *la Religiosa,* Heavenly Treasure, Heavenly Teacher, Venerable Teacher . . ."[2]

Why did he give her these titles?

Pietro reiterated her supernatural prerogative of living on communion alone and her role as intercessor, thus returning to the point at which he had begun. The inquisitor, too, circled back, veering abruptly toward the concrete, to humble everyday reality. He asked whether, since they had come to Venice, he had brought food to his two companions, and if so, what kind.

From his brother's shop he had brought Don Pietro cutlets and salami.

How often, and how much salami?

Twice, two salami each time.

Did he know whether Maria had eaten any of the salami?

Not as far as he knew, although on Sunday, the day after they were arrested, he had gone into the woman's room and had not found the salami he himself had put on the beam, nor, looking under the mattress, had he found the slices of headcheese he had wrapped in paper.

Aha, the inquisitor may have sneered, that's a fine answer! The two Pietros must have been in secret competition, first to provide food for the saint, and now to remove all suspicion from her! But unless the double, linked imposture had been agreed on between them, one of them must be innocent. One had placed the salami and the sliced headcheese in the two hiding places, and the other knew it. Hence one of the two had lied—undoubtedly Father Pietro, the first to be

2. [*Religiosa* in the sense of nun. Since the primary meaning of *maestra* ("mistress") would have a misleading connotation in English, the term is translated here as "teacher."]

interrogated and, even more important, the first to have the opportunity to get the woman off the hook. But if the priest had not stashed away the food for his own use, Palazzi had brought it into the house only for Maria. On the other hand, if outsiders did indeed visit the house, the two men had hidden the food for themselves in what they thought to be the safest places.

Then the inquisitor passed, apparently without a logical connection, to a different issue. How long had it been since he made his confession, and who was his confessor?

Palazzi was excluded from saintliness precisely because of his conscience, which was not as clear as those of his two associates—and although he did not realize it, this gave him an advantage. He had confessed two weeks earlier at San Bonaventura to a friar he believed to be the father provincial.

Again the inquisitor shifted gears. Hadn't the unexpected departure of two men in the company of a young woman not related to them scandalized anyone?

There was no scandal of any kind because they were known in the village.

And during the journey?

If anyone asked, they said that they were two brothers and their sister.

Fra Ambrogio jumped at the bait. If they claimed to be siblings in the inns as well, what sleeping arrangements were made for them?

Equaling and perhaps surpassing in candor his master the priest, Pietro replied, "We almost always slept in two rooms. When we were put in one, however, there were two beds, one for the woman and the other for the priest and me."

To this, the inquisitor of one of the darkest periods in history, who by virtue of his office and his mental furniture was supposed to see corruption everywhere—even more than his confreres of two or three centuries later—found nothing to object.

6

WITHOUT REMORSE

*T*he good Don Iseppo Rizzo showed up again, "spontaneously," at the Holy Office on 2 March. If his reappearance was really unexpected, now that the trial was under-way, it was a real piece of luck for the inquisitor. It may well be, however, that Fra Ambrogio had let out the word about the alleged fast. If so, when it reached Calle della Stua, it probably evoked a com-ment along these lines: "With all these mouths I have to feed, I'd like to learn how to get along without eating!" That was all it took to encourage Don Iseppo's penitents to confide in him further.

The priest made clear what he had to report. "I'm here to tell you what else I've learned from the women." Positioned at the crack in the door one Saturday morning after the domestic communion had been introduced, Antonia had observed that Donna Maria "held in her hand a platter or bowl with something in it that appeared to be pasta, sprinkled with cheese from the way the strands looked. Maria was pulling the food out and eating it."

Antonia had seen her eat twice more, on different days. The first time she put bread into her mouth; the second time she was carefully chewing the salami brought her by Pietro Palazzi from his half broth-er's shop. The girl did not know whether on the day the woman ate bread she had taken communion. Antonia was certain, however, that on the morning the woman broke her fast with salami she had received the eucharist. That the woman's countryman and onetime fellow in-habitant of the house had visited her at such a special time had sur-prised her. Antonia's sister, Meneghina, had seen the Bergamasque woman, seated, stirring some food. From the movement of her hand, which rose to her mouth and then descended, Meneghina surmised that she was eating, although the crack was too narrow to permit observing her mouth.

Don Iseppo was about to leave, but then he hesitated and stopped. He had something else "of considerable importance" to reveal. Very likely because he too had tasted the bitter pleasure of putting a colleague in a bad light or hitting a man when he was down, the inquisitor encouraged him. He asked him whether the priest now in jail had been present while the woman was eating.

Rizzo did not know. What he had to say, alas, concerned a quite different matter. One of the Bellini sisters had told him in the confessional that twice, before communion, while the woman was taking the box from around her neck, she had seen her touch the priest—"I don't know whether reverently or affectionately, once putting her hand on his shoulder, another time resting her head on his shoulder." For the moment, however, this information did not interest Fra Ambrogio.

If we grant, although it has not yet been proven, that Maria was feigning, eating must have been for her the gravest of transgressions, and hence the physical act of which she was particularly ashamed. On the three or four occasions—actually two, as we shall see later —when she put food to her mouth, she had the impression of being spied on. Antonia, called back to testify, had definitely seen her eat once, the Saturday before she was arrested, an hour after Nones, that is, around four in the afternoon. She held a platter full of pasta sprinkled with cheese and mixed with nice pieces of meat. With a fork she speared the biggest pieces, using a spoon to scoop up the rest. She had carried the hot platter from the kitchen, and the priest was present. He was keeping watch, walking back and forth, on pins and needles.

Perhaps Maria felt insecure in that house. The next time she seemed to be avoiding the crack in the door. Were the Bellini sisters fighting over who got to watch? Antonia, the younger, was also the more aggressive and inquisitive. She discovered a peephole in the beams on the staircase and watched the woman descend it with half a salami in her hand.

A third time, back at the usual observation post, the girl saw that Pietro who wasn't a priest give the woman some salami, a bag, and some pieces of bread, which the woman hid partly under the straw mattress and partly in the blue trunk. "Having taken one of the bigger pieces of bread, she brought it to her mouth and took a bite, putting the rest in her purse. And she gave the said Pietro, who was present, the two other pieces."

The fourth and last meal was allegedly consumed during the afternoon of the same day, which suggests that if Maria took nourishment, she did so at irregular intervals but abundantly. The younger Bellini saw the woman open the trunk, take something out of the paper package, and head down to the room below. Antonia heard her close the door on the stairs and stay there for awhile, from which she inferred that during that pause the woman was eating.

Meneghina, too, could testify against the foreigner, although she was a scrupulous girl, disinclined to jump to conclusions. She was twenty-eight and unmarried. At that advanced age, according to the social norms of the era, she was unlikely to find a husband, particularly because she was very short in stature. She had to make do with the lower part of the crack, which was even more narrow, through which she could see their neighbor, even when she was seated, only up to the chin. Therefore all she was prepared to say was that the woman's hand, with something white between her fingers, rose repeatedly in the direction of her mouth.

The sisters had not a word to say about the affectionate gesture to which their confessor had alluded. Respecting the modesty of marriageable young women, Fra Ambrogio did not raise the issue.

Confronted with all this evidence, the priest would surely decide to admit that for far too long he and his disciple had been playing an ingenuous and impious game. On 9 March, therefore, the inquisitor, certain that he could now overcome all the obstacles, had Morali brought back into court. Fracassini exhorted him in a fatherly manner to tell the truth, which up to this point, as the record showed, he had always denied. Father Pietro claimed to want nothing more, "preferring death to telling a lie."

They got off to a bad start. Following the rules of procedure, which demanded patience and detachment, Fra Ambrogio forced himself to begin by asking whether during the journey from Zorzone, and then in Rome and Venice, he had seen the woman eat.

Since Morali could tell that behind the interrogator's apparent coolness lay a certainty based on evidence and reasoning, he decided to make a small concession. Although he had never seen the woman eat or drink, on occasion she had asked his permission to wash her mouth with water and wine, assuring him that she would do so in secret. The defendant, aware that his cooperation was being well received, forged ahead, assuming that the inquisitor was giving him an opportunity to confute evidence against him which unfortunately seemed convincing. It was also the case, he admitted, that every so often, in order to conceal her privilege better, Maria had made a show of taking bread and putting it in her mouth.

The inquisitor leaped at the contradiction. What? On the one hand the priest's protégé washed out her mouth in secret so that her prerogative would not be questioned, while on the other she pretended to bring food to her lips in order to be considered a normal person? The witness must reconcile these two conflicting statements.

The poor priest, having cut the ground out from under himself, made a feeble attempt to recover his footing. He had had to reveal Maria's privilege to the proprietors of their various lodgings, whom he had urged to keep it to themselves, but the servant and apprentices around these houses knew nothing about it. Therefore, in agreement with their hosts, she made it appear that she was eating. This had occurred, for instance, when they were living near the Servite monastery.

That could be, the inquisitor conceded, and no one denied it, but in other lodgings after they had left the one near the Servi, the woman Maria had been observed eating: one Saturday, around four in the afternoon, in his presence.

Feeling the blow, Don Pietro thought for a moment. Then he recovered his certainty, buttressed both by his unshakable faith in his pupil and by the long duration and the approval from on high of their enterprise.

Let him listen, then, to what a witness had said. "The first time I saw her eat, she had a platter of pasta abundantly sprinkled with cheese. And she had a fork, with which she ate the bigger pieces from the platter, using a spoon for the smaller ones." The witness stressed that "she carried that platter of food upstairs, in the presence of Father Pietro, who was with her, and he went back and forth like a lookout to see whether anyone came upstairs. I didn't see the priest eat. They were talking together in such low voices that I couldn't understand them. The priest was watching the woman eat."

Very much taken aback, Don Morali was forced to come up with some kind of immediate response. The best he could do was to inquire why should they believe a witness in preference to him, or them, who were people completely devoted to serving God? That deposition was absolutely false; whoever made it was lying. He was certain that Maria had never eaten, especially not, as someone had falsely claimed, in his presence.

Take note of the fact, the inquisitor insisted, that the witness knew what kind of food and the day, hour, and circumstances in which it was consumed. It was the defendant, therefore, who was testifying falsely.

The priest, who did not hesitate to throw onto the scale his own good faith, stressed that he alone had firsthand knowledge of the alleged episode. Naturally Maria, who cooked for him and for others in the house, carried around bowls and platters, and sometimes she amused herself by pretending to eat along with them. But neither of the two could doubt the other because they were both totally observant of what they called "the gift of faith."

The inquisitor, endowed with greater patience and expertise than we, could probably enter more fully into the reading of the priest's inspired biography of Maria. The friar was in fact the ideal reader of this document, set down in rough, reckless Latin by her master, whose work had been rudely interrupted by the arrival of the arresting officers in Calle della Stua. Don Morali, both credulous and skeptical—like members of the lower classes when they pursue unaccustomed objectives but at the same time do nothing without a reason—had written the biography to serve as a proof of sanctity or an attestation of good conduct. Following the pattern of similar texts that had crossed his path, put together in most cases by the confessors of holy women, it was subdivided into numerous short chapters, each illustrating a particular virtue of the woman: from devotion to wisdom, from humility to fortitude. Recurring so frequently as to disarm suspicion was the word "love," always capitalized. Attached to it were adjectives like "immense," "infinite," "boundless." These were often employed in the metaphor of the sea or ocean, causing the text to founder in that "infinite sea of love" in which today's teenagers and writers of popular songs swim. It was a phrase he had heard which had become part of their private lexicon. The same was the case with the more rational concept "gift of faith," about which the inquisitor continued to be curious, perhaps not satisfied by the explanation Pietro Palazzi had provided. The man who had coined it could surely explain it better.

"As I understand it, faith is a substance of the divine promises made by the Lord in the Gospel, and thus I have taught it, with the proviso that one ask only for things to His honor and glory and in conformity with His will."

Fra Ambrogio thought he could understand it better through its not infrequent applications. For instance, had the box containing the communion wafers been blessed by a bishop?

No, he himself had blessed it.

By what authority, given that he did not have a license to do so?

He had blessed it as one blesses the bread and wine of communion, without any other intention, having been thus inspired.

Had he believed, then, that it was legal for a Catholic priest to consecrate hosts privately without saying mass, administer communion outside a church, and give a woman the holy sacrament to wear around her neck?

Because of his faith in God, Father Morali had believed that he could do all this. These were things he had requested and obtained through prayer, to the greater glory of God, and they had not caused him to feel "any repugnance." Had he felt repugnance or aversion, the slightest tinge of guilt and remorse, he certainly would not have continued to do such things, "but I would rather have died." One of the proofs that what he was doing was right was the special reward received by Maria, who also served God in complete serenity of mind.

Cause and effect continually changed places; the vicious circle remained forever closed. The inquisitor read to the priest the Council of Trent's condemnation of the concept of faith endorsed by the heretics. But he did not realize that he was following a false lead. Father Pietro, Maria, and their disciple—even if, or rather because, they endorsed everything the Church proclaimed—sought to find within the Catholic system some outlet for their frustrated ambitions. Palazzi sublimated his unreturned love for Maria by laying it at the feet of the

Mother of God. Janis, who had not been able to become a nun, was trying to become a saint. The priest, disliked by his colleagues and not well thought of in the episcopal curia, arrogated to himself a power reserved to the higher ranks of the clergy. Blocked from a normal, gradual spiritual ascent, they aimed at the exception which tests the rule, and their consciences, the only guide in ethical decisions, supported their effort. One might say that they were operating not in the shadow of clandestinity but rather in the bright light of relentless and even somewhat treacherous competition. Unlike the Protestants, who trusted in prayer to break free from the bonds of the Church's precepts, our three threw themselves into the Church, hoping for signs of celestial favor.

For the inquisitor, on the contrary, the Church stood above the individual conscience. It received inspiration and assistance from the Holy Spirit. It could not err. Whoever stood outside it had fallen into heresy, or else had made common cause with the Devil.

The Church, the priest agreed, is supreme on earth. But was it not possible for God, Lord of both heaven and earth, to make exceptions for those who served Him without asking questions?

The inquisitor, who also served Him blindly, shook his head. God does not play favorites. He has delegated the Church to represent Him.

In effect, our three bewildered protagonists, irregulars rather than rebels, had knocked at the wrong door, unaware that special concessions, particular favors, and exceptions are in reality the rewards arbitrarily granted by the powers of this world. They are to be obtained not just by serving those who possess power but by doing something for them above and beyond the call of duty, which is almost always something questionable. Since Morali, Janis, and Palazzi had nothing to offer but submission and renunciation carried to an extreme, all they could hope for was a divine privilege.

Father Pietro was about to be conducted back to jail. Before he left the room, the inquisitor unexpectedly asked him, perhaps not without a touch of irony, whether his form of belief and practice was designed to bring about a new Church, a new concept of holiness, a new faith.

"No, Most Reverend Sir, I have not claimed anything of the sort. I have only seen to it that Maria was provided with her supper in the way I have explained until her status in the Church was made manifest."

In that case, as we can see in retrospect, he should have tried to ingratiate himself exclusively with the representatives of the Church and to operate more adroitly, for men are shrewder than God.

7

THE SEA OF LOVE

*S*ince we can probably exclude the possibility that in the jail of the Holy Office, two detainees of different sexes could meet and consult each other, it is tempting to suggest that Maria Janis, in addition to being a woman with keen intuition, possessed talents as a medium. At the beginning of her second encounter with the inquisitor, sounding almost as if she had overheard Don Morali being questioned, she volunteered that on the last Wednesday of Carnival, the Madonna, appearing to her in a cloud, had informed her that her master, her inestimable Don Pietro, "was being assaulted by the Devil," but that Holy Church could not be tricked and therefore she should not worry. A few hours later, Maria, too, would have to battle with the Devil.

Fra Ambrogio listened to this monologue without interrupting her, then remembered his job. The first thing he wanted to find out was whether the priest had taken control of the woman's will, and if so, to what extent she was aware of it. Why, he asked, had she submitted herself so completely to the curate that she followed him to Rome and then to Venice and shared "hearth and home" with him?

Maria revealed nothing new. Her response could well have been attributed to Morali or Palazzi, like a school exercise or an artisan's product. In order to fulfill the will of God, they had agreed to leave their home, their relatives, and other worldly things. She had never seen anything wrong with that.

Explain more fully, the inquisitor went on, the purpose of the white garment made in Rome, which she was to put on at the end of her road.

Her earthly journey was to conclude right here in Venice, where, when it pleased the Mother of God, she would be dressed in the special garment by none other than Her Divine Son.

Maria therefore envisioned finishing her days in Venice, the city in which she would be recognized as a saint. But given the fact that she shut herself up at home, declining to go out even to take communion, how did she expect that to happen? It seems reasonable to surmise that she and her master had awaited in vain a foreordained encounter with someone highly placed in the Church, perhaps even the pope. Having ended up among the anonymous masses in Rome—where, however, their moves had taken them closer and closer to St. Peter's—and then in Venice, the two may have decided to let themselves be drawn into the net of the Holy Office, whose members included, as we have seen, the patriarch of Venice and the papal nuncio. The inquisitor, the gray eminence in the trio of ecclesiastics on the tribunal, now gave her a full opportunity to reveal herself. For what purpose would the Lord vest her in the white garment?

This could have been the moment she was waiting for. During the trial, however, Maria was dressed in prisoner's garb, and her explanation consisted of the same old story the inquisitor had already heard. She replied that the white robe, along with the other garments, belts, and stoles, were ordered for her by the Virgin to manifest and honor her privilege of living on communion alone.

How, the inquisitor inquired, had she received this privilege?

Always, ever since she was a little girl, she had had a particular devotion to the sacrament of the eucharist. Some time after she had vowed to subject herself completely to the will of God, the idea "passed one day through my heart" of taking no nourishment other than the bread of heaven. Then, just after she had taken communion, she felt herself fall into "an ocean of infinite love." She began by fasting for a week, then skipped communion and began to eat again. But that day she was so ill that she felt constrained, and at the same time encouraged, to extend her fast to fifteen and then twenty days. When she stopped, she immediately became ill again, whether from eating food or forgoing the sacrament. Hence she decided to renounce forever all food and all drink and to take communion every day.

For how long had she not eaten and taken communion daily?

For five years she had not touched food and had taken communion every day, except on Good Friday, when the celestial supper of the day before continued to produce its effect, maintaining her strength.

What had she done during the journey, and then in Rome and here in Venice?

She had always lived on the bread of the angels. For example, in coming from Rome to Venice, she boarded a boat at Rimini around noon, after having taken communion in that city. The next day they anchored at another port, where she got off the boat in order to receive the sacrament from Don Pietro and then went aboard again. On the following day they arrived in Venice, where the first thing she did was to go into a church to consume her holy meal.

And after that in Venice?

Maria immediately realized what lay behind that question and was prompt to cover herself. Not even in Venice had she eaten or drunk, although on occasion she had pretended to do so in order to conceal her privilege.

The Holy Office, however, the inquisitor told her, knew that she had been seen eating several times, not pretending to eat but doing so on the sly. Therefore she had better tell the truth.

She had certainly not eaten or drunk.

A witness had sworn to having seen her do so one day, the inquisitor proclaimed. He proceeded to read her the testimony concerning the pasta sprinkled with cheese.

We have no way of knowing what Maria's immediate reaction was, except that she did not pause to think. Her prompt response, like others which she made later, was typical of a woman of the people: "Anyone can say whatever they please." If she had appeared to be eating, she had been either pretending or joking.

The defendant was lying, the inquisitor insisted. First of all, since there was no one else present, there was no need to pretend. Furthermore, "in a matter as important as this, one shouldn't go around joking."

At this moment Maria may have realized that she had gained a small point. By calling the matter serious, the inquisitor was not excluding the possibility of her living on communion alone. She was probably gratified, but the need immediately arose to account for the possible presence of outsiders in the house before whom she had been constrained to pretend. Had she known about the crack in the door which had brought about her ruin, she could have turned it to her advantage, claiming that she pretended because she knew that she was being spied on. In fact, it almost sounds as if she did know about it. She replied, "I suspected that someone saw me pretending to eat, and

I saw them. That's why I didn't pretend for the aforementioned reason [as a joke]." That is, discovered while she was pretending and aware of the fact, she was obliged to continue doing so, not in jest but rather to keep up the impression that she ate like everyone else and thus maintain the secret of her privilege. But the women in the Bellini family surely would have been at the crack when she took her clandestine communion, and hence Maria would have had to show that she was fasting at all times.

The inquisitor, too, may have fallen for a moment into this equivocal trap, for he pressed her to guess who might have seen her.

Since the devout woman from Vertova did not suppose that walls in Venice had ears and eyes more keen than elsewhere, she searched exclusively among the circle of acquaintances who had been in the house. It could have been Pietro Palazzi's brother Giacomo, some of his apprentices, or Peverada the grain merchant.

How had she accomplished the feat of pretending to eat and getting people to believe her?

She held food in her hand and brought it up to her mouth.

This corresponds to what Meneghina Bellini had testified. But the inquisitor wasted no time in reading Maria another passage from the deposition of Antonia Bellini. "After dinner on the same day, when she was in her room, I saw her take some of the stuff wrapped in paper that she had put into the trunk that morning, which appeared to me to be meat. She went into the other room, and I heard her bolt the door on the stairway. Since she stayed there for a little while, I surmised that she was eating."

Maria's reply demonstrates bold, even provocative assurance, as if she were boasting about her ability as a simulator. "Anyone can say whatever they think and like, but no one could have seen me."

Fra Ambrogio accepted the challenge and had no difficulty in entrapping her. The same person who had seen her take communion in her room—an act the defendant herself admitted—had also observed her eating.

The woman defended herself like someone who had run out of convincing arguments. "I can only tell the truth, as I have done, even if the whole world says the contrary." And in a new burst of provocation, she went as far as to put the Inquisition on guard against liars:

"Holy Church cannot be deceived, as you'll soon find out."

8

THE BERGAMASQUE COLONY

*F*or the moment, let's leave sanctity and prison.

The little villages of the valleys and the Oltre il Colle basin were in ferment. Following the news that the two fugitives, the priest and his protégé, had been arrested, about twenty people received an order to present themselves to the Holy Office in Bergamo. The appearance and interrogation of witnesses, most of them from Zorzone, proceeded slowly. From Venice came complaints from the inquisitor general, who urged that the transcripts be sent on. His delegate felt the need to justify himself: he should not be criticized for laziness or negligence in this case because he was having a good deal of difficulty getting the witnesses, particularly the women, to come down from the mountains, a journey of from sixteen to twenty-four miles.[1] In the meantime, Fra Ambrogio decided to call the Bergamasques resident in Venice who had had contact with the two defendants.

All young men, they were well established in the city's retail trade. They were in business for themselves, with their own shops, specializing in sausages and grain. Their inspiration was the fabulous career of the merchant Pietro Tiraboschi Bombello of Serina, who had made his fortune in the city on the lagoon. His estate amounted to forty-five thousand ducats, part of it bequeathed to the convent under construction which Maria had wanted to enter. After business hours these immigrants had relatively little to do with native Venetians. Instead, they stuck together and maintained ties with their home villages. But when they returned home, putting on their city airs, they found no accommodations suitable to the social status they had achieved with their pluck and hard work in the capital.

1. [A Venetian mile (1,738.674 meters) was somewhat longer than the modern English-American mile (1,609.344 meters). Angelo Martini, *Manuale di meterologia* (1883; rpt. Rome: E.R.A., 1976), 817.]

Our three pilgrims, as we have seen, had also come to Venice, a city which must have known something about sainthood and other celestial triumphs, at least through the work of the many painters who had been born or settled there (among them a native of Serina, Palma il Vecchio). In Venice, they were certain, they could count on Giacomo Panighetti, who had been miraculously cured by Morali, and secondarily on Giacomo Palazzi, Pietro's half brother, to provide hospitality. When they disembarked from the boat that had brought them from Rimini, they knocked on the door of Panighetti, who had a sausage shop in the parish of Santa Margherita, not far from the docks on the Zattere.

The welcome they received was typical of an emigrant from the country who treats all visitors from back home as family members, feeling obligated to give them his own bed while he slept on a mattress on the floor. Besides, it was cold, and it was Lent. The pious travelers, Panighetti assumed, had come to Venice to prepare themselves properly for Easter. The two more important visitors had access to the two bedrooms in the house, which they shared with the master of the house and his wife. (Pietro Palazzi went to stay with his half brother.) There they remained, the two men in one room, the women in the other, for about three weeks, until Easter.

To demonstrate his gratitude to the curate, Giacomo Panighetti would have continued indefinitely to give up his matrimonial bed. Four years earlier, reduced to a desperate state because he could not retain food in his stomach, he had turned to Don Pietro, who had made him kneel down and recite the Hail Mary and had then asked him whether he believed that God had the power to cure him. Panighetti responded in the affirmative; the priest gave him the benediction and told him that his illness was "cut out." From then on, he did not suffer further from any sort of indisposition. God had cured him for the faith he had manifested in Him, and Don Pietro would accept no payment for his ministrations. For this reason Panighetti was glad to welcome the priest into his home in Venice and also to provide his meals—meals for Don Pietro only, because the woman never sat down at the table. It was said that she didn't eat, and in fact he had never seen her put food into her mouth.

If she had wished to, the inquisitor indelicately inquired, would she have had an opportunity to eat on the sly?

Certainly, but to his knowledge she had never done so. She left the house every morning to receive communion, and according to the priest, she lived on that alone.

What sort of impression had the fact that the priest was living with a woman made on him?

"I never formed any sort of bad opinion of them."

The master and his disciple did not want to inconvenience the good couple any longer. They decided to leave before they had worn out their welcome. In the meantime, Giacomo Palazzi had bought an apartment near Santa Maria dei Servi in Cannaregio, on the edge of the Ghetto, and before furnishing it and moving his wife and their children from his brother-in-law's house, he camped out there with his half brother Pietro. Pressed by Pietro to take in Don Pietro and Maria too, he finally gave in. Morali sensed that the enterprising Palazzi, a sausage-maker in business for himself, was not a generous man, and that when his feeble-minded half brother had unexpectedly turned up, he had seen him only as a potential employee. Therefore the priest assured Giacomo Palazzi that they would not stay long, and that he need not worry about their meals: the woman, in fact, didn't eat. Never before had Maria's privilege had such an enthusiastic reception, so much so that their host extended it also to the priest, who in order to eat had to draw on his savings.

Giacomo the sausage-maker had these guests under his roof for five months, from Easter to the Assumption of the Virgin in mid-August. He could honestly say that he had never seen the woman eat except once, when she took something from a plate and put her hand to her mouth.

In his long experience, the inquisitor had observed that stingy people are often well informed about matters that do not concern them. He also realized that at the Servi the vagabond couple had been almost forced to pack up and leave. But given the tie of blood between the sausage-maker and one of the three runaways, he might be able to pick up some interesting information, particularly concerning the past. Why, he asked Giacomo Palazzi, did he think his brother had left home and followed the two?

From what he had been led to believe ten years ago, Pietro was thinking about leaving the world and joining a religious order.

Had Maria lived in their house in Zorzone?

Yes, but by then he was already in Venice. He heard about it from others.

Before going to live there, had the woman known or been friendly with anyone in the house?

Not as far as he knew. His father had taken her in because she was from Vertova, a town only twelve miles from Zorzone.

Did she work in the house?

He didn't know what kind of work she might have done, since his father was a weaver.

In his indefatigable service as an inquisitor, Fracassini had also learned that old men whose sexual powers are on the wane are often desperate enough to try anything in the attempt to satisfy their urges—and that they almost always ruin themselves without having succeeded. Giacomo, however, did not pick up the hint. He did not know why his father had kept the girl in his house, nor whether he had charged her rent. Most likely he had taken her in out of charity, because the son had heard that she lived in a little room below ground, a type of cellar reached by going down ten or twelve steps. (As a child, he must have counted them many times.)

The young man inspired a feeling of masculine solidarity in Fra Ambrogio. For the first time the master of sacred theology mentioned the word "love" written in lower case. Did the sausage-maker know by any chance whether there were "young men" in his father's house during the time Maria lived there, and "did you know whether any of them was in love with her?"

Living with his father were the youngest brother, Giovanni, already married, and Pietro, who from that point of view was not too swift. Hence he really did not know who could have been in love with Maria "with bad intentions."

Why had the priest left his post in Zorzone?

To be free of responsibilities: the priest was a man without mercenary motives. But Giacomo had also heard that he was disliked by other priests in the area.

For what reason?

Again according to hearsay, because many people went to him

to be blessed. He also conducted a school of Christian Doctrine for the children and ran the Confraternity of the Belt, which the faithful from other parishes joined, paying a subscription fee.

Finally, what opinion had Giacomo formed of this priest and his disciple?

Called on to express a personal opinion, Palazzi the sausage-maker reverted to his habitual stinginess. He held the priest to be as good a person "as any other," and the same went for the woman, although he judged it impossible that she didn't eat, since he had once (in five months) seen her put her hand to her mouth.

In the apartment, empty except for a little secondhand furniture, Don Morali was visited by two of his former pupils in the school of Christian Doctrine: Antonio Peverada and Domenico Calvi, both around twenty-five, who had left Serina and Cornèl respectively as adolescents and had remained close friends. Although the first traded in grain and the second ran a paint shop (and hence was commonly known as Menego dai Colori), they lived together, co-owners of a small apartment at San Mattio di Rialto. In response to the continual complaints of Palazzi the sausage-maker, who after all had bought the new house to make a home for his wife and children, Don Pietro decided to ask for refuge with these two young men, who were clearly well disposed toward him. Out of pique, in order to demonstrate that one can get more help from outsiders than from one's own relatives, Pietro Palazzi left his half brother's house and again became the chaperon, servant, and follower of Morali and Janis.

Peverada was capable of speaking grammatically and with a certain elegance; he and his friend Menego signed their names with an ostentatious flourish. They were the advance guard of the era, with relatively open minds or at least the desire to learn new things. For the young grain merchant with his own shop at the Ponte delle Beccarie, well established now that Venice was importing most of its grain from the agricultural hinterland, the parish of Zorzone seemed "small and insignificant, with about thirty hearths, and the curate is removable," as well as being low-paid.

The inquisitor tried to sound him out. Perhaps he remembered the curate's having exorcised and blessed people?

By the time Don Pietro began to gain fame as a healer, Antonio Peverada had left the village. Still, he had heard that the priest did not charge for his services and that he exhorted those he helped to thank God for having granted them His grace.

What had been said in Zorzone about the departure of the priest with the woman?

Peverada had been in Bergamo during the past Lent. The people of Zorzone were unhappy that Don Pietro and Maria had ended up in prison, since they had left the village only to do the will of God. In the city, on the other hand, rumor had it that the priest had been arrested for going off with the woman.

During the five months, from August to December, that the two had lived in his and Menego's house, how had they comported themselves?

The two businessmen were also short on space, but they had given their good rooms to Maria and the curate and moved with Pietro Palazzi into the hall. At mealtimes they sat down at the same table, except for Maria, who didn't eat and only occasionally joined them, a little removed from the table, without ever taking any of the food that she, taking turns with Palazzi, cooked.

Could he say whether the two "associated very closely with each other" while they lived in his house?

He and Domenico went out to conduct their businesses and Pietro also left the house frequently, so the two remained alone.

How did he think they passed that time?

Sometimes the woman sewed shirts for her own use, and once she made a pair of sheets for them. But for the most part they read the Office and the lives of the saints. At certain hours she stayed closed in a room, giving no indication of what she was doing. The priest, too, stayed in his room to read his breviary, write, and pray, kneeling in front of a stool.

In these successive reports of a devout, chaste life, it is obvious that for the inquisitor, every detail assumed a disproportionate importance and aroused his suspicion. Hence Fra Ambrogio, who had probed into more noteworthy and sometimes disconcerting aspects, now inquired about mundane details, such as how the woman had obtained the cloth for the shirts.

"When I saw her sewing shirts, they were not new ones; she worked with old shirts, altering them."

Thus this fissure, which might have led who knows where, was also promptly closed. Perhaps Fracassini realized he had gone astray into a realm of reality from which he quickly withdrew, betraying a sudden lack of interest and barely disguised uneasiness.

In December Father Morali made arrangements for their fourth and last move, this time on his own initiative. Peverada and Calvi were not deliberately making them feel unwelcome, nor were they politely but unsuccessfully concealing the fact that they were discommoded by the presence of three guests. What probably happened was that the curate from Zorzone and his disciple inferred from the attitude of the priest at San Giovanni Elemosiniere the possibility that he might betray them. Don Pietro had no difficulty in obtaining help from the amiable, prosperous Menego, who bought an apartment in a part of the same quarter further away from churches and therefore less reputable.

After they had moved into the two little rooms in Calle della Stua, the young paint-seller accompanied the priest on his excursions around the city. Father Morali was bashful only up to a certain point. Besides being less than diplomatic with his colleagues, he was notably complaisant toward people in power. Such an inclination often dampened his sensitivity toward the less fortunate and those who found themselves in difficulty.

True, he did visit a porter from his mountains. And through "money given to Signor Lorenzo, a wool merchant with a shop on Rialto," he had one Giovanni Battista Viani, a merchant in Campo dei Fiori in Rome, give poor Annamaria Casolina, in danger of being forced into prostitution, fifteen *giulii* a month. As if to demonstrate that our reckless priest always worked within the bosom of the Church, however, his friend Menego told how one day two men from the Grisons, a father and son, had turned up at the house to obtain from the healer-priest a remedy for their wife and mother, who had been bewitched. Don Pietro, surmising that they were not Catholics,[2] had told them that he had to know what their religion was before he could give them "certain water drawn from the Gospels." In effect, he showed them to the door.

On the other hand, when he heard that the Duke of Modena lay ill in Venice, he insisted, with the bravery of the timid and the bravura of a second-rate actor, that he be conducted to the sick man's bedside. He did not consider it an imposition to make Menego accompany him twice more to the residence of the Modenese ambassador and wait for hours while he had a confidential conversation with the duke. At the end of one of these visits, the curate from Zorzone was taken aside by a gentleman who offered him five gold *dobli,* which at first the priest refused to accept. Then, when he was told that they were given to him out of charity, he replied that for the sake of charity, he would take them. On their way back home, Don Morali told Menego that the duke had invited him to Modena, but he had declined the invitation because it was God's plan that he stay in Venice.

If God had not lied to him, it must have meant either that the trial was about to take a new turn or that the Lord fully acknowledged the office of the inquisitor and in secret was already collaborating with him.

But before moving to the branch office of the Inquisition in Bergamo, let us hear one more interesting and new tidbit that Fra Ambrogio managed to extract from Menego. One of his apprentices, a boy of twelve or thirteen, often went to the apartment in Calle della Stua, sometimes staying overnight in the priest's room. Since he did not know of Maria's privilege, his presence could have induced her to pretend to eat. Father Morali had told Calvi one day that he had taken the woman away with him because she was a saint. He had decided to leave the village because the bishop had ordered him to bring to an end the influx of so many pilgrims into Zorzone. Unwilling or unable to maintain that promise, he had concluded that it was better to depart, to become a pilgrim himself.

---

2. The area of the Grisons in southern Switzerland, then a subject territory of the Swiss Confederation and now a canton, had been predominantly Protestant for over a century.

II

MARIA TAKES FLIGHT

9

THE MODEL PARISHIONER

ord of the arrest and imprisonment of Don Pietro Morali and Maria Janis, which had occurred as Carnival was getting under way in Venice, filtered into the Bergamasque valleys during Lent through two different channels. Notwithstanding the fact that the cold kept people indoors and occupied in penitential practices, it spread rapidly throughout the region and evoked comment even in Bergamo.

The news was brought to Zorzone by Antonio Peverada, the young grain merchant, who, like many emigrants, preferred to return home during this season. Though winter in the mountains was long and hard, the very bleakness of the snow-covered landscape meant that what happened in these months was indelibly inscribed on people's memories. Visiting the Palazzi house, Maria's home for two years, where old father Giovanni continued to live with his son of the same name and daughter-in-law, Peverada attributed the arrest to the fact that consecrated communion wafers had been found on the woman. The arrest and the reason given for it did not particularly surprise or scandalize anyone in the family. The new pastor, Giovan Maria Grassa da Oneda (rector in the full sense, not merely a paid curate), was especially curious to learn more. Even though he had inherited from his predecessor the good will of the more prosperous and devout families, he had not found it easy to move into Morali's place. It was three years now since the beloved priest and his disciple, accompanied by poor Pietro, had left, and in Grassa's judgment their journey could have ended only as it had. Their departure from Zorzone had been an attempt to escape from the control of the Church, which in the meantime had had ample opportunity to cast its net and pull it back in. For Grassa's parishioners, on the other hand, the fact that Maria had been carrying on her person the only food with which she claimed to nourish herself was considered natural enough. Both the old people and the young in Zorzone, though accustomed to the close and surely innocent relationship between the priest and the devout woman, considered that for the ecclesiastical authorities, their going on the road and probably living in the same room was sufficient reason for the arrest. Peverada himself reported that the two had expected it, leading us to suspect that Don Pietro, besides being afraid that Rizzo would denounce them, had intentionally brought their presence to the attention of the Holy Office, supported and perhaps even encouraged by Maria, who was not averse to transforming her own room into a theater.

The other channel by which the news traveled ran through the Val Seriana to Maria's birthplace. In the piazza of Vertova a priest from the nearby village of Gorno who had just returned from Venice spoke freely about what he had heard there. Two of his listeners took it upon themselves to go up to Colzate and burst into the house of the Janis family (here called Janes or Anes) in order to be the first to inform Maria's mother, brother, and younger sister. Crossing at Oltre il Colle, the two rumors merged to such an extent that they almost canceled each other out. They were authoritatively confirmed, however, first by the rural dean of Dossena during his frequent visits to the parish priests most interested in the news and then by the arrival of the guards bearing the summonses to those wanted for questioning in Bergamo.

From early May to the beginning of June, now that good weather provided no excuse for not traveling to the regional capital, some twenty people, in groups of three or four, went down from the two valleys, headed for the episcopal palace in Bergamo Alta. On the road they exchanged recollections and opinions, thereby testing but also influencing one other. Let's see what we can learn from their depositions.

Until she was twenty, Maria had lived in Colzate in a family even poorer than the others. Her father, Giovanni Antonio, whose daughter by his first marriage had married and moved back to the parish of Vertova, had taken a second wife, Lucrezia de Caporal. A sickly man, he did not pursue any particular occupation. The family members who put bread on the table were the mother and her children, Giovanni Battista, Caterina, and especially Maria, who tirelessly spun wool both on a spindle and on a wheel. She also surpassed her parents and siblings in her devoutness and observance of the principles of the Christian life. She attended church on the required feast days in order to hear mass and vespers, participated in Christian Doctrine classes, and took communion not only on the first and third Sundays of every month and all the feasts of the Virgin but also frequently on weekdays. At home she was assiduous in attempting to help the less fortunate. When she could take a little time from her work, she read books of prayers. Maria's hard work, however, did not improve the family's fortune. As soon as her brother and sister were old enough to fend for themselves and no longer dependent on her for their daily bread, she began to think about becoming a nun. Her aim was to enter the cloistered convent of Dominican sisters intended for poor women which was under construction in Serina Alta.

The young curate of Zorzone, Don Pietro Morali, often visited the Janis family. Born in Zambla, where he had left his small inheritance to his brother, he was a friend of Maria's father, who had worked as a day laborer for his family, and therefore he was often asked to stay for supper. Maria, intent on pursuing her vocation, grew to like this thirty-year-old priest, so fervent and disinterested in comparison to most of his peers, who had earned a reputation for holiness and had drawn many faithful Christians from surrounding parishes to his little church, which was known as far away as the Bergamo plain. Her affection was accepted and returned by the young priest, who was equally fond of the whole family, and therefore it grew and came out into the open. In contrast to other conscientious, exemplary priests, he had a certain glow of passion in his eyes, which he had to reveal at least partially lest it burn out of control. Because all the members of the Janis family considered themselves his favorites, he could allow himself to visit them more and more frequently.

Maria asked her father to intervene with Don Pietro, in the hope that the priest could influence an elderly nun of Serina, the most likely candidate to become prioress of the convent, to pave the way for Maria's acceptance. We can interpret her plea as an exploratory, maybe even provocative maneuver. Although his normal inclination was to avoid direct requests, Don Morali did not know how to refuse this one, but he managed to gain time by making an alternative proposal.

In order to gain entry into the convent, the young woman had less need of a dowry than of adequate preparation. First of all, it would be desirable that she learn to read the Great Office, that is, the breviary normally reserved to priests. He would be glad to help her when he came down to Colzate, but the task would require practically full-time concentration and dedication.

Maria countered the priest's ambiguous mixture of hesitancy and optimism with a bright idea, pursued with bold determination. Realizing that she could earn her living just as well in Zorzone as in Colzate, she made contact with a distant relative, a hermit in the convent of San Patrizio in Vertova, who on his rounds begging alms had become familiar with all the houses and even the abandoned stalls and huts in the area. The little man with red hair was by no means discontented with the vocation he had chosen because of the independent life it afforded him. Hence he encouraged Maria in her choice. In the outskirts of Zorzone it would not be difficult to find at least a temporary accommodation in the deserted farmhouse belonging to one Colombo, a member of the parish council and therefore devoted to the curate.

Maria took her small store of belongings, including her distaff and spindle, and, accompanied by her mother, went up to Zorzone at haying time in mid-June, thus confronting Don Pietro with a fait accompli. Or according to another version, furnished by Morali's most determined opponents and unsupported by the facts, it was he who had her brought into his parish, charging his brother from Zambla to escort her to Zorzone.

When we land in a new place, the first person to welcome us often turns out to be our worst enemy because he or she is reluctant to acknowledge that we can make it on our own. The mother and daughter found a place to spend the night a few doors from the church with an elderly unmarried woman who lived alone and put up beggars and wanderers in her hovel. Living in the center of town with time on her hands, Margarita Castellina kept a close eye on what went on in the village and commented on everything she saw and heard with the pungent sarcasm of an old maid. Probably because in the past she had not dared to complain about sexual abuse and other forms of mistreatment, she continued to be the butt of jokes and insults launched by her neighbors.

When Maria showed up at the rectory, Don Pietro's first reaction was that her presence was too obvious and visible, and above all too close. But the veiled suggestion that she come to Zorzone had actually been his, and the girl had obtained the consent of her family, whose confidence in him was clearly manifested by the imploring expression on Maria's mother's face as she more or less entrusted her daughter to him. The curate quickly reviewed the possible lodgings in the village, thinking more of getting his protégé out of Castellina's hands than of actually finding her accommodations. Maria herself mentioned Colombo, and Don Pietro jumped at the suggestion. Colombo's abandoned farmhouse was off the beaten track, near the declivity that ran up toward his native Zambla, and its proprietor was the delegate responsible for the administration of church property in one of the zones into which the parish was divided. The good parishioner was not at home—he spent the summer months in huts up in the mountains tending his flock and cutting wood—but his wife did not hesitate to give the curate the keys to the outbuilding. Now that the aspiring nun had a roof under which to pray and work, her mother could go home to her other children.

Gian Domenico Colombo, who referred to himself as a "fugitive"[1] because he spent a third of the year in the forests and the remaining months "minding his own business," was the first person to aid Maria in her work as well as giving her lodging. One day he passed by the hut, isolated in a meadow on the hillside, where he had left some of his tools and part of last winter's hay. Seeing her—so young, all alone, and dressed in black—he was moved by tenderness and perhaps something more. He offered her the best kind of wool to spin, paying in kind for the finished product with flour, butter, and various kinds of cheese, including the mascarpone extracted from curdled milk before it is turned into ricotta.[2] Others followed his example, partly for charitable reasons and partly because Maria was a good worker who soon obtained a spinning wheel in order to work more efficiently, as she had done at home.

1. ["Ucello di bosco": literally, "bird of the woods."]
2. [Mascarpone: a form of cream cheese; ricotta: the Italian equivalent of cottage cheese, most often used in baked lasagne.]

She turned the single room into an abode poorer but more inviting than that of Castellina, whose company she increasingly avoided. This nosy gossip was her exact opposite, as well as the biggest obstacle to her leading a retired life. As a humble outsider, Maria's immediate object for the moment was to become a model parishioner. During the brief summer season, women were employed in the fields to rake hay, cut barley, and weed buckwheat. Most of the men and boys, if they were not still mowing the fields, had gone up to herd the flocks of cattle and sheep in the pastures on Mounts Menna and Arera.

Maria went to weekday mass, at which she was often the only one in attendance. Since she helped the priest move the missal and handed him the cruets of wine and water at the offertory, she was practically a concelebrant.[3] They remained together after communion, while she was still immersed in the prayer of thanks and listening to the good advice given her by the Lord whom she had just received, Who was still warm and vibrant in both their souls. Sometimes she stayed for a long time in the pew, and Don Pietro, prolonging his own concluding prayers, waited for her to finish before offering the empty chalice. The sounds of their voices, devout sighs, and footsteps alternated and merged, amplified in the silence of dawn, which inside the church retained the cool and the intimacy of the night. Then, when she knelt at the confessional, Maria spoke as if to herself, baring her heart and accusing herself of omissions which weren't really sins and of legitimate temptations such as thinking ill of the inquisitive old woman who cast spells over the coals and made snide comments about her assiduous attendance at religious ceremonies. She took part in the children's Christian Doctrine lessons, for she still had a good deal to learn about the basic principles of her religion, but in her case every article of faith she heard was transformed into prayer.

One day, when Don Pietro had to absent himself in response to an urgent summons, he assigned Maria to carry on with the Christian Doctrine sessions. She aimed to make sure that even the shyest and laziest children reached the level of their peers, so that they could

3. [Moving the missal from the Epistle to the Gospel side of the altar and handing the priest the vessels containing white wine (which he alone consumed) and water with which to wash his hands were functions ordinarily performed by altar boys. Only since the Second Vatican Council have women in some parts of the Roman Catholic world been permitted to assist the celebrant.]

make a good impression on the curate. She took them to her own lodging and had them repeat the catechism after her, following her distinct pronunciation and intonation of the words. Because the children were still too young to work and would otherwise have remained unsupervised, their parents were happy enough to have them go, particularly since the aspiring nun often fed them bread and mascarpone. The alms she received now served as compensation for her main activity, and her work of spinning became an almost embarrassing sideline. Don Morali, absorbed with more important duties, finally turned the entire Christian Doctrine course over to her. He remembered, however, that this neophyte teacher had come to Zorzone to learn. The reading of the Great Office of the mass, as priests did, was both an obligation and a prerogative of one who had already dedicated herself to teaching others. The young woman from Colzate was satisfied with managing to read the Latin without understanding it. For her it was a set of incomprehensible but completely religious sounds, a language reserved to the consecrated for direct communication with God. Gian Domenico Colombo, when he stopped by his outbuilding, observed the curate as he instructed his disciple. "Each of them had a book in hand. One said one verse and the other the next, and if Maria made a mistake, Don Pietro corrected her."

To the people of Zorzone Maria became "the nun" or "the religious": since she was preparing to enter a convent, they assumed that she must already be committed by a solemn vow. This circumstance, linked to the open protection the curate was now giving her, preserved her from the unwelcome confidences of the old women, as well as from the attention of the bolder young men, to whom she looked nothing like a girl destined for the convent. Ten years later, testifying before the Inquisition, her landlord remembered her with masculine sympathy that had perhaps lightened the burden of the long hours he spent in the mountains. "She was a pretty young woman, plump, with a pink and white complexion—in short, a pretty, lovable girl, who spoke and behaved well. She seemed to be between eighteen and twenty, and everyone around liked her."

Don Pietro didn't share their opinion, or else he didn't pay attention to the looks of his pupil, marred by a small deformity which only he noticed and which would eventually disappear. What concerned him were her soul, her piety, her dedication, which alone could render her worthy of his regard and serve as a substitute for her physical appearance. Maria totally accepted his conception of her. The more she prepared herself for the spiritual life, the more definitively she renounced the satisfactions of the world, thus competing with the priest called upon to function as her stimulus, her supporter, and her source of inspiration.

10

THE VOLUNTARY NOVITIATE

*I*n 1627, responding to a request from a group of citizens, among them two members of the Palazzi family and a Peverada, the general of the Augustinian Order had authorized the foundation in Zorzone of the Confraternity of Mary Virgin of Consolation of the Holy Belt of St. Augustine and His Mother St. Monica.[1] During Morali's tenure as curate, the confraternity gained new adherents in the neighboring parishes. They flocked to the village to buy the leather belt which members fastened around their waists. Our aspiring nun joined as well. The Virgin Mary and the two saints, mother and son—a trio which came to represent or even to substitute for the official Holy Trinity, to which the parish church was dedicated—were implored for favors which the original statutes had not promised. But Morali, who was following the example of St. Augustine, not of the Augustinian friar Martin Luther, urged the unfortunate favor-seekers to have faith: if it was the will that inspired people to achieve their wildest dreams, it was faith that could accomplish miracles. As one witness testified, "they came every day in the hundreds . . . , lots and lots of them, yes, sir."

This malnourished flock, most of them infirm, summoned their last reserves of energy to climb up to the village tucked into the slope of Mount Menna. All they needed to feel relief was a little attention. Don Pietro reassured them by citing from the Gospel: "Ask and it will be given to you, knock and the door will be opened." No one, he insisted, should make the mistake of thinking that credit was due to

---

1. The founding Palazzi were Pietro fu [son of the late] Zoane and Pietro fu Giacomo. *Compendio degli obblighi, indulgenze e vantaggi degli ascritti alla Confraternita della Sacra Cintura nella Parrocchia della SS. Trinità in Zorzone* (Bergamo: Pietro Greppi for the Curia Vescovile di Bergamo, 1868), 2. They were undoubtedly members of the family with whom Maria lodged in Zorzone; the latter was probably the elder Giovanni Palazzi's brother.

him. He was only an intermediary who would not be needed if they could find for themselves the way to absolute faith, which involved the gradual attainment of a state of joy, accompanied by a loss of skepticism—and, we might add, of self-control.

In the exultant village the role of model parishioner, even one promoted to the position of collaborator with the curate, no longer satisfied the young woman from Colzate. She was less and less enthusiastic about the approaching prospect of shutting herself up in a cell in the Serina convent. Her relative the hermit, who could not stand the restrictions of a monastery, may have played a part in this progressive renunciation of her highest adolescent aspiration. He came to visit every so often and stayed to dine with her. According to a witness, he was "a thin little man with a ruddy complexion, who not long ago was imprisoned by the Inquisition here in Bergamo."

Maria felt called upon to isolate herself from the world and make other sacrifices. Her assertive character and humble origin allowed her greater freedom of choice than that afforded a well-born nun, above all the opportunity to obtain frequent verification of her special state that came through contact and comparison with others. Her idea of monastic life involved breaking with her ordinary everyday existence, visibly overcoming it, and little by little achieving the exact opposite. Even the little miracles performed by Don Pietro were coming too close to being everyday occurrences. What was needed to proclaim unambiguously the glory of God, to translate the principle of faith into a manifest certainty that would astonish even its enunciator, was something extraordinary, truly exceptional.

Maria read the lives of the saints. In her damp, dark hut, forgetting to eat while rushing back from religious services to spin piles of wool, she confused faith with will, special grace with the prize automatically earned through blind dedication. Tired and weak, she received the first indications that she was on the right path. She spoke aloud to the Virgin, adding to her prayers phrases from the dialect of Colzate, which she sometimes translated into standard Italian as if to prompt the response which was struggling to emerge from within her. It was the voice of conscience, no longer under her control and often contrary to her will.

Her mother and sister frequently came to see her. First of all, they would light the fire, which Maria, who had built herself a fireplace, now left cold for days on end, even though the wind blew in gusts of snow and the roof behind her hut backed up on the path. After poking around in the cupboard, not satisfied with the cheese, mascarpone, and lumps of butter they found there, they opened the sack of flour brought from their home further down the valley and made a thick soup which warmed and quieted the stomach. They were surprised when Maria stopped eating after a few spoonfuls and emptied out her bowl. They reported how much money they had managed to put aside during the past few weeks and told her about the neighbor woman who had finally married the miller of Casnigo. They asked her what was delaying her entry into the convent but didn't wait to hear her answer because they were already snoring on the straw pallet laid out on the dirt floor.

Thus Maria's new life was interrupted by an everyday reality of which she no longer felt herself part. The presence of mother Lucrezia and sister Caterina, even when they were silent, and the disorder they introduced to her lodging led her to petty thoughts, to inept attempts to resume her dialogue with the Virgin, to a bad conscience prompted both by her having broken off her tender, intimate relationship with the Mother of God and by her urgent desire that her family leave as soon as possible. Suspended between two ways of life and forced to pretend in order to repudiate the one and hide the other, she came to realize that everything ordinary people did was aimed at satisfying the demands of the body. They worked to appease their hunger, then slept in order to return to work and refill their bellies. It was no different for the rich: they spent most of their time and money arranging longer and more elaborate meals, and they invented all kinds of amusements so as to enjoy them more. People were slaves to themselves before they became slaves of their masters or superiors, who took advantage of this internal servitude to hold them more easily in subjection. Even those leading the religious life, persons devoted to God, not excluding Don Pietro, had to interrupt their prayers and works of charity to sit down at table. And the sick, most of whom had stomach complaints, came to be blessed so that they could go back to stuffing their bellies. She began to wonder whether anyone had ever thought of eliminating the root cause of our animal nature, of the unworthiness of our real selves.

Maria came to feel that the fullness and sweetness that overcame her when she took communion were the exalted, noble alternative to the satiation of the stomach and the filling of the bladder and bowels that followed the consumption of normal food. Living on communion alone and eating had very different consequences: the one resulted merely in physical weakness, while the other poisoned both body and mind. She would try to maintain herself as long as possible in the state of beatitude that lightened her and seemed to free her from her body. The final prize was assured: Christ Himself had promised that whoever eats the bread of the angels will remain full. All that was required was faith and constancy. God became Man for no other reason than to turn the conventional order of things upside down and to offer the lowliest of the low the opportunity to attain humanity's most cherished aim, that of liberating itself from the last chains of the human condition and making itself one with Him.

Maria's voluntary novitiate, her retreat into the desert, lasted more than four years, during which time the pretty young woman, plump, pink, and white, became "thin, withered, and swarthy." One month during the fifth year she prolonged her usual Friday fast through Saturday. On Sunday there were several masses as well as vespers, with the usual concourse of pilgrims, and she did not return home until evening. She made a new sacrifice, and the next morning she confessed to Don Pietro that she had fasted since the previous Thursday.

The curate, though not surprised by the test his pupil had given herself, interpreted it as a challenge which humbled him and elicited his expression of admiration. At the same time, however, he felt himself in the clutches of a sort of holy terror. He sensed that the young woman was capable of going much further and putting him, who was indirectly responsible for her doing so, in the position of no longer being able to judge her. Feigning concern for her health, he made himself reproach her for the first time and announced that he would grant her absolution only on condition that she start eating again. Then they would see. Maria, probably inferring the conflicting emotions running through her confessor's mind, obeyed, but vomited up the food. She returned to the confessional with her face still contorted.

Don Morali, gravely implicated in both the credit and the responsibility for her condition, put himself even further on the defensive in an effort to suppress his insidious sense of satisfaction. It must be a trick of the Devil, he told his penitent, mounted without her realizing it. The young woman had never seen her friend look at her with a greater mixture of affection and severity. His behavior, seemingly a declaration of solidarity, might well signal disdain, dislike, and anger. Maria broke down in tears. He could say anything he wanted, but not that her sacrifice was serving the Devil's purposes.

This was a legitimate, quite natural protest which hit its target. Don Pietro found himself in the position of appearing to have repudiated his penitent and thus making his authority over her odious. He proposed a pact: she could receive the holy bread as long as she promised to eat at least once a week. Then, again, they would see.

Maria agreed to the compromise, it seems, only because, feeling bound to give precedence to the voice of the Virgin, she believed that she was simultaneously obeying the will of the curate, who summoned all to faith in God. In reality she had no desire to eat even on the evening of the seventh day, when a few hours of sleep lay between her and another week of uninterrupted and permitted celestial nourishment. She wanted to lie or refrain from raising the issue of the time limit, but those seven days were even longer for the master than for the pupil. When he summoned her into the confessional, she admitted that she had disobeyed him.

Morali suddenly became aware of a possibility which he had never before seriously considered. These weeks of fasting could be entered on the list of little prodigies that distinguished his ministry from all the others in the district. Might not the quantity and variety of merits which God had chosen to dispense through him also demonstrate that heaven looked on the little mountain parish with extraordinary favor? This latest development, however, was too great a privilege, one for which he could in no way take credit, both because in Maria's case he was no longer exercising a determining role and because the benefit had seemingly matured here on earth and was producing more suffering than serenity or joy. Could it be that the young woman was trying to imitate him, to please him, and hence to outdo him by adopting an objective and a strategy that were all too human, or rather feminine?

On the point of denying her absolution, Don Pietro yielded to the temptation to take the measure of the extraordinary feat, thus deluding himself that he was controlling it though not actually opposing it. He gave Maria another week, with the absolute proviso that she resume eating at the end of the fifteenth day.

The days passed, one identical to another. Maria's face was thinner every morning. But the light in her eyes, growing larger in their sockets, especially after communion, seemed to signal a certain joy, which in fact was nothing other than satisfaction that they had reached an agreement. When, on the fifteenth day, the girl revealed her obedience by confessing that she had taken food, he felt relief but also disappointment and renewed concern. Because he had twice bent to her will, the young woman anticipated that the period of her fast would be extended further, and he was no longer in a position to refuse her.

11

COMMUNION AS A DRUG

*A*n unrelated event lifted from the curate's shoulders a responsibility that had become all too heavy. Word arrived from Colzate that Giovanni Antonio Janis had died. Maria went home, having been led by Don Pietro to understand that a long stay with her family would be good for her.

Since she had no concrete commitments in Zorzone and had been more or less encouraged to stay away, it would have been impolite to leave her mother and siblings right after the funeral, but she was not inclined to take up her old life. For mass and communion she was prevented from going down to the Vertova church, an edifice surrounded by a colonnade that rose up over the roofs of the large town. Some months before, the parish priest had clashed with Morali about the curate's providing spiritual counsel to the parishioners of Vertova enrolled in the Confraternity of the Belt. In this controversy, which had ended up in the episcopal curia and had been decided in favor of the parish priest of Vertova, with Morali required to pay him damages, all the inhabitants of Zorzone had lined up on the side of the curate. They had gone so far as to appeal to the papal nuncio in Venice against "an imprudent condemnation issued by the curia of Bergamo, under the presidency of Gian Ballo Lavezzano, Vicar General of Bishop Luigi Grimani, in favor of the parish priest of Vertova, who challenged the right of the priest of Zorzone to administer the holy sacraments to the members of the Confraternity of the Holy Belt in any place whatsoever and without conditions." In this suit brought by the priest of her home parish, Maria had quite rightly seen his annoyance about the removal from his control of a parishioner dedicated to the religious life, one who in the hands of a foolish but fortunate exorcist risked the deformation of her own faith and vocation. No one had asked her to intervene in the dispute, but her aspiration to render her new parish and its pastor even more deserving of special recognition had grown by leaps and bounds.

During the days following the burial of her father, Maria became aware that the antipathy toward Don Pietro that had infected the curate of Colzate included her as well, as he demonstrated in the form of disappointed affection so typical of country people left behind without any previous warning. At mass on weekday mornings she was the only person in the little church to recite the confession as soon as the celebrant had raised the chalice to his lips. Therefore, with a sigh, her former pastor decided to open the tabernacle. One day he summoned her to confession, and she promptly refused. The priest took communion by himself and quickly finished the mass.

Maria encountered similar difficulties with her family. Her fasting, first hidden and then disguised, evoked concern and then ever more cutting comments poking fun at her pretension in trying to raise herself from the condition in which she had been born—one she now felt she had been condemned to. As a consequence, the voluntary novice had to yield at least to some extent, and she found it easier to sit down at table with others in the house than to reveal the secrets of her soul to the ill-disposed curate. Constrained to renounce her celestial supper and eat the soups which Mamma Lucrezia tried to make appetizing, Maria fell into a state of spiritual prostration destined to grow and fester the more her body was satisfied. The successful renunciation of four long years seemed to be going up in smoke, Morali stayed away, crowds continued to flock to Zorzone in spite of her absence, and she felt herself assaulted by delayed pangs of gnawing hunger.

She was so cast down, hopeless, and disappointed, especially in herself, that the Devil found her easy prey. "She went to bed," her mother recalled, "and couldn't move. She cried out, saying that the Devil was attacking her, and I realized that she was possessed, because the Devil was making her dance. I asked permission from the curate to summon a Carmelite father from Albino, called Fra Disdotto. I sent my son Giovanni Battista with a horse to bring the father here, and so he came. . . . Maria was in bad shape; by then she couldn't move her hands or any other limb, and she lay in bed groaning. When the father had exorcised her, she immediately got out of bed, cured, as if she had never been ill, and she immediately picked up her spindle and began to spin."

In the bosom of her family she could allow herself to pretend that she had been cured, just as she had had to act out the internal battle, which had not in fact ceased, with the Devil, who she thought was angry about the interruption of her deliberately indefinite fast.[1] For another two months or so she stayed at home, eating, drinking, and spinning, with Zorzone always on her mind. Don Pietro did not come to see her. She interpreted his long silence as meaning that he was forcing himself not to contact her.

One day he arrived, on the pretext of passing through on his way to Bergamo. He hardly recognized her. She felt the ground shake under her feet and her eyes blurred, for the unexpected return of a loved one after a long absence makes time pass more quickly than his continued presence. Maria suffered a new and more violent attack by the Devil, from which she emerged covered with bruises. Was the prime exorcist of the region constrained to use physical force on a particularly recalcitrant devil, or did the possessed woman, so as not to be left alone again, go to the extreme of throwing herself against a wall? Whatever the case may be, during the crisis she spoke with another voice, saying words unworthy of her, which made her spiritual father realize that she had been reduced to such a state for having reneged on her special relationship with God.

They returned to Zorzone. To make up for lost time, sustained by the reserves of nourishment she had taken, she threw herself into a long fast, a final trial run. Don Pietro was not pleased. He urged her to respect their agreement, so as not to create problems for him that he could not resolve on his own. Sooner or later, he realized, he would have to inform one of his superiors, perhaps the bishop, as he was required to do in unusual cases. Once again Maria read his mind and followed his instructions as she saw fit, obeying the will of God and of her conscience—and every so often, when her confessor insisted, the law of nature. Her body, how-

1.[See below, chapter 18, pp. 135–37.]

ever, having been denied, satisfied, and then denied again, would not cooperate. "After I had ordered her more than ten times to eat," Morali would later report to his superior, "she ate, but in less than half an hour, unable to keep the food down, she vomited, fainted, and grew pale."

The young woman from Colzate had definitely given up the food of mortals, a renunciation which in the long run leads to death and in her case seemed likely to prove fatal in a much shorter time. Don Pietro, observing her closely to see whether the phenomenon occurred as it had before, was now prepared to support her, though without completely abdicating his responsibility and power. But his pupil required more active cooperation. She was not prepared to admit that her spiritual guide, who was also a healer, could limit himself to a passive role. In order to renounce human food completely, Maria needed to feed more frequently on the bread of the angels. Aware that priests were allowed to celebrate several masses in one day and naturally to take communion every time, she surmised that such a privilege was denied the common people precisely because it was granted to those who were ordained. What had once been her ultimate aspiration now presented itself to her as something like an earthly license to sustain herself on the great flight she had undertaken. She did not dare to ask her confessor for this unusual concession. Instead, she played games with time.

One Sunday she took communion at the last morning mass and returned to the altar Monday at dawn. Don Pietro, who noticed, reminded her that at least twenty hours had to elapse between one communion and the next. With a mixture of incredulity, caution, and faith, he began to watch the clock. Under such close surveillance, Maria felt her resistance crumble in the face of this challenge. She had to fight the hours, the minutes; time seemed to stand still. The urge for food itself was now supplanted by the much more compelling desire for the symbol. She had taken communion early in the morning. Now it was not yet evening and she felt that she couldn't go on. She couldn't concentrate on her prayers. She tried to go to bed; she got up again. Only a few minutes had passed. She tried to pull herself together until at least a few hours had passed and the village fell into darkness. Then, like a drugged woman, she dragged herself uphill between the low, gray houses, gagged at the sound of the cows chewing in their stalls, and with a supreme effort managed to pull herself up to the priest's door.

"An hour before the end of that day, she came and knocked at the door of my house, barely managing to stand, and said to me, 'If you don't give me my communion, I'll die.' When she told me that, I responded that I was troubled, and she replied that I mustn't be afraid, that it was God's will that I give her her supper. I took her into the church and administered the sacrament of the eucharist to her. She immediately revived and regained her strength. If I remember rightly, she told me that day that before receiving the holy sacrament, she had been so weak that she couldn't say the usual prayer."

Father Pietro surrendered. From then on he gave her communion every day and, in secret, three other times per week. It was the infraction of the rules, or the privilege, that she had wanted for some time. Master and disciple had forged a bond which excluded physical contact but might prove even more dangerous than the ordinary sexual relationship sometimes formed between a priest and a female parishioner. From this point on they would devote all their time and strength to sublimate, but at the same time legitimize, this relationship.

12

THE GOLDEN PHASE

*J*ust as if they were involved in an ordinary love affair, the first thing the two had to do was reduce as much as possible the distance that separated them. Maria could no longer isolate herself in Colombo's house outside the village. Now that her body, sanctified by the uninterrupted presence of the holy sacrament, had become a living monstrance, to be jealously guarded and put on display only at the proper times, she needed to be taken care of, assisted, and guided. The church or the rectory would have been the ideal residence for her, but her moving to either one would be seen as a profanation that would evoke cries of sacrilege or scandal.

Not far from the two buildings, standing on high ground so that it dominated the entire village, was the house of Giovanni Palazzi, the only private residence in the village that bore some resemblance to a public building. There the elder Palazzi, a leader among the village notables, maintained his weaving business, in which the entire family was employed. On holidays the Palazzi "kept a sort of tavern" to accommodate the growing crowds of confraternity members and other pilgrims. The house had one space that the family no longer used: "a vaulted room completely underground[1] except on the east, where there is a balcony that looks into our tavern, and on the west is the door; when you come up the stairs, you look out on the main street." In that room Maria could remain rigorously secluded and completely independent. For the first time, when he proposed her to the Palazzi family as a potential lodger, Don Morali found a way of introducing his protégé that would prove very effective, then and in the future, mainly because he raised the matter in a humble and low-key fashion.

---

1. The term in the local dialect is *silter,* the sound of which the notary of the Holy Office in Bergamo tried to reproduce with *ciltro.* The word is probably of Celtic origin.

Her hosts needn't worry about her meals, he assured them. She didn't require any because she lived on communion alone.

In the cellar room Maria slept on a typical medieval peasant bed: three supports, some planks laid across them, and on top a mattress filled with dry leaves, for which she had two sets of sheets and two blankets. Her clothes, kept in a chest, included her habitual garment, a black robe with wide sleeves resembling a nun's habit. Among the members of the Palazzi family she associated most closely with her contemporary Caterina, wife of the younger Giovanni, who was the brother of the sausage-maker in Venice. Having assumed control of the little family's businesses of weaving and inn-keeping, he lorded it over his half brother Pietro, born from their father's previous marriage.

At first none of them believed in their guest's special privilege. The young wife tactfully demonstrated her willingness to help out Maria by pressing her to accept half a dozen eggs, which she could use as she chose. Caterina, who often visited Maria in the cellar room, was the first to become convinced of their lodger's extraordinary status, so much so that very soon she became Maria's open ally.

Maria attempted successfully to follow her master's example by employing on Caterina the supernatural powers that naturally accompanied her privilege. When the mistress of the house mentioned being afflicted by a mysterious malady that troubled her particularly at night, her guest had her lie down on the mattress, made the sign of the cross over her, and persuaded her "not to pay attention to her illness" because now it was cured. With this weight off her shoulders, Caterina could not conceal her relief from other members of the family. Since she had no other way of showing gratitude to her guest, she invited the holy woman to warm herself at their fireplace. Maria took a spindle from one of Caterina's and Giovanni's young daughters, demonstrated skill at the loom, and talked about one thing and another, "such as that weaving was easy if the wool was spun well, 'I've had a chat with so and so,' and other things of that sort, the way women talk among themselves."

Donna Caterina mentioned that she had dreamed about her father, who had died some years before. She wondered whether the dream meant that he was in purgatory and begging her to have a mass said for him. With a smile and a nod, Maria confirmed her surmise. Then the young master of the house asked what had become of his poor dead mother. Appearing to inquire of those on high rather than looking directly into the world beyond the grave, Maria stated that she too was in purgatory. Next it was Pietro's turn to interrogate her. For the eldest brother, who had been orphaned at a tender age, had never really bonded with his father's new family, and had not formed one of his own, his mother, Giustina, mowed down by the plague along with hundreds of other people in the area, was more than just a ghost who appeared occasionally in his dreams or came to mind when others talked about their dead parents. Therefore he waited until Maria went back down to her cell, which he had not previously dared to enter. When he went in, he was guilt-stricken about invading her privacy on the pretext of a fond memory. But any other excuse would have been even less plausible.

With this discreet, pious man Maria probably did not have the courage to pretend. Since she did not hesitate to repeat herself, revealing that his mother was also being punished for her sins, it is clear that she was sincere. The Church in that era could hardly have given him a different answer, and Pietro believed her. What must have seemed more out of the ordinary to him, as it does to us, was that within the narrow horizons of their static world, a young woman whose inclinations were so similar to his own and therefore was so well suited to him should have come to live under his very own roof.

Pietro Palazzi, too, intended to dedicate himself to the religious life, but his aspiration, unlike Maria's, was not a point of arrival but a strategy of escape, as shown by the fact that in secret he composed verses. His romantic bent ran ahead of his religious sensibility, leading him to see in the "marriageable young woman" a gift from fortune rather than an agent of the divine plan. Sounds and silence, shadows and light, their echoes and refractions intensified his feelings, which were sublimated only in part by their common religious longings.

Maria interpreted Palazzi's attitude as "great affection." As far as his half brother was concerned, however, Pietro was only a dead weight on the family economy. "He fooled around so much; instead of working, he wasted his time with her, which made me so angry I didn't even talk to him." But from the point of view of Maria's younger sister, who came to visit her in her new home and stayed for months, it was a question of love. How could she tell? "From the loving attitude that Pietro had toward my sister Maria," who limited herself to "demonstrating [or perhaps feigning] a friendly attitude toward him."

On the conscious level, it was easier for Maria to deal with the first man who had fallen in love with her than with God, even though she had been in close contact with Him for at least five years. Pietro, on the contrary, having yielded to human love, had no qualms about pursuing his beloved. Just as the curate had done with her, Maria neither rejected him completely nor misled him. In her view, their relationship had to remain and be consummated exclusively on the spiritual plane. His company and his devotion would be useful to her. If necessary, he could be the focus of any suspicion and facilitate her contact with the consecrated Pietro. The priest, to whom Maria, short on sins, reported everything, was well aware of this fact.

From then on, the priest's visits to Maria's cellar room to discuss the lives of the saints, tutor her in the reading of the Great Office, and engage in mental prayer became much more frequent. The house of her suitor, which functioned also as an inn, reached by a steep path bordered by stakes implanted in the adjoining meadow, was the only place where master and disciple could be alone, even at night. When she wanted to return the priest's visits, all she had to do was call on her escort.

Thus Maria started going to the rectory. Since she often cooked for the priest, she could conceivably have slept there. Her virtue and her disinclination to lose it, however, were threatened by the pantry, not the bedroom. She set the table for guests, who often included Pietro's old father, but as soon as they sat down to dinner, she returned home.

In the Palazzi household she achieved a better footing with the real man of the house, the younger Giovanni, when the captain of the militia arrived in the village square to select by lot the men to be enrolled for a long term of service (up to fourteen years) in the territorial defense force. Caterina's husband asked her whether he would be drafted. Maria encouraged him not to worry because his name would not be drawn, and her prediction proved correct. From then on, she was sometimes present, standing near the table, while they dined. When she was invited to sit down and keep them company, she responded, not exactly to the point, that they were eating "dirt and filth." In her cellar room she now held classes in Christian Doctrine for a small group of boys and girls—*putti e schiatte*[2] in the words of grandfather Palazzi, who, having been born in the previous century, was not ashamed to employ vivid terminology that had fallen out of current usage. When he testified, he could still remember the sound of the teacher's voice as she catechized the children: "Speak up,[3] tell me how many holy sacraments there are; speak up, say what extreme unction is." For him, Maria became, among other things, "the one who made the children speak up."

It seems clear that Maria had adapted herself to her new situation in the spirit of obedience, and that she had not cut her ties with her own family. She played hostess to her sister, who was curious about everything, lively, and above all hungry. During Caterina Janis's visits the cellar room was perfumed, or profaned, with the food which the younger sister went upstairs to prepare in the kitchen of the other Caterina. Maria, far from calling these dishes "filth," was occasionally indulgent enough to season them and even stir them in the frying pan with her own hands.

Don Pietro, who had been so diffident and distant in the past, now had complete faith in his pupil and fully acknowledged her gifts as a medium. He gave her room for maneuver and even receded into the background. Perhaps he realized that in a parish of a few hundred souls, two saints might be too many, and therefore he contented himself with serving merely as the agent of God, or John the Baptist. He went so far as to put in her hands the life of his married sister in Valpiana, "given up on by the doctors and all swollen up inside." Sent to her bedside, Maria was put to a test which signified how much trust he had in her. Far from repudiating her master's method, to which she added a bit of her own character and imagination, she commanded the malady to "cure itself" by virtue of the most holy name of Jesus. Then she put her hand on the sick woman's stomach and, lo and behold, Morali's sister recovered.

This episode, however, did not signify the curate's definitive retirement in favor of his disciple. In tandem with Maria, Don Pietro continued to bless the crippled and those possessed by the Devil. To

2. Boys and girls; the latter term, *s'cete* in the local dialect, derives from *maschiette* ("little boys" with a feminine ending).

3. ["Di' [dir] su," which could also be translated as "come on!"]

cite again the words of the elder Palazzi, "some were cured and others weren't." In contrast, Maria, a careful and cunning observer who could empathize with those unfortunates because she too had battled with the Devil, never failed. Nor did she limit herself to cures. During a storm, she took a hailstone, crushed it, and throwing it to the ground, ordered the tempest to change direction. Pietro's half brother, normally cautious and preoccupied with mundane matters, swore that "the storm immediately ceased, and this I saw with my own eyes."

On Sundays the narrow streets of the village could hardly contain the crowds. Few saints have had such satisfaction during their lifetimes. Although Maria could have resumed eating without damaging her reputation, she didn't feel the need. Furthermore, she was well aware that her living on communion alone constituted, especially for her master, the hinge on which the new prestige of the parish turned. She charitably recycled the loaves of sugar, cheeses, and baskets of pears and chestnuts given to her in gratitude and homage by donating them to those pilgrims whose only way of expressing their gratitude for being cured was to thank the Lord. Through the enterprising mistress of the house, who often diverted the curate's clients to her, she also received offerings of money, which she promptly turned over to the church. The only gifts Maria kept for herself were handkerchiefs, shirts, and "big white aprons." Over her black habit she wore a white stole, folded across her chest, which descended to the ground; on her head was a veil of white lace. Her dress was termed "extravagant" by Caterina's husband, who had never seen any woman, much less any nun, decked out in such a way. Despite her total fast, which Don Pietro not only acknowledged but bragged about to his close friends and whispered about to others, Maria became just as "plump and pretty as she had been, returning to her former beauty."

With the rather portly attractiveness of a satisfied woman, Maria now seemed to embody not the Church of Lent, Christmas, or Easter, but rather the Church Triumphant, celebrated during the summer holidays of Pentecost and Corpus Domini. When during Sunday mass she moved forward from her pew to the altar to receive the sacrament, the crowds parted on either side of the nave, holding their breath as if they were about to witness a miracle or a stupendous magician's trick.

Her success gave her self-confidence, but from our point of view the new Maria seems less human and sympathetic than the emaciated, troubled one. On one occasion she strikes us as positively odious, like Don Pietro in his future encounter with the two men from the Grisons shown the door in Venice—and that was not the only time he pulled rank. Responding to the snide insinuations of Margarita Castellina, who reminded her who had first taken her in, recalled how miserable she had been then even though she was eating, and made fun of her playing the saint, Maria did not hesitate to accuse the old woman of witchcraft. Morali, too, was so overconfident that he threatened to "make an example" of Margarita, that is, to denounce her. If he had been above criticism like his colleagues in the area, he would have been taken at his word, and the old woman would have been at some risk, since witches at that time were still being driven out of the woods into church squares to be prosecuted.

Padre Pietro, however, was less interested in proceeding against witches than in making the most of the favorable situation by presenting the jewel of his parish to notables and other influential friends outside the parish. In a house in Serina Alta, Maria even had a private conversation with the prospective prioress of the convent she had wanted to enter. Much impressed by Maria's appearance and speech, the nun could hardly believe that she might have had this treasure in her charge. But to the young woman from Colzate, her former dream now seemed only an adolescent infatuation. Don Pietro, on the other hand, saw an opportunity to draw profit from the encounter. Anxious to gain supporters on higher levels, he attempted a reconciliation with the other pastors in the neighborhood, hoping perhaps that his unchallenged success would mitigate their envy.

The rector of Serina, Father Girolamo Carara, showed great interest in Maria's privilege, especially after the prioress had told him that "talking with that young woman gladdened her heart and kindled in her the flame of divine love." When he asked his colleague to introduce him to Maria, Don Morali invited him to come to Zorzone whenever he wished. Once Carara crossed his threshold, however, Father Pietro backed off, saying that he was sorry not to be able to grant his colleague's wish, but that it was Wednesday, a day which Maria devoted exclusively to prayer. The crestfallen visitor speculated aloud as to whether it might be advisable to write the life of such an exemplary parishioner, to which Don Pietro retorted that someone was already doing so, leaving no doubt as to who the biographer might be.

Morali had no better luck with Father Giuseppe Valle, the chaplain of Valpiana. Managing to encounter Maria in the rectory of Zorzone, Valle observed that she seemed to be very much at home there, since she went upstairs and closed a door behind her. The visitor easily obtained more damaging information from Margarita Castellina, recently tarred with the brush of witchcraft, who had been observing all the alleged cures with considerable skepticism. According to her, though Morali exhorted the pilgrims to thank God for the benefits they had received, claiming to want nothing for himself, he suggested that whoever wished to make an offering leave it in the rectory or with Pietro Palazzi, who then secretly passed it on to Maria. Maria in turn gave some of these donations to her mother and sister when they came to visit. The priest from Valpiana was especially curious about the devout woman's publicized prerogative of doing without ordinary food. Learning that the old gossip Margarita shared his incredulity, he allied with his colleague from Oltre il Colle to conduct a clandestine inspection.

When the two priests traveled up to Zorzone at dusk, just after the evening bells had rung, luck came to their assistance. In the kitchen of the rectory a group of people were eating dinner. Don Valle and Don Giuseppe Merloni had no trouble recognizing the voices of the curate, old Palazzi, his son Pietro, and Maria. No question about it, they were eating: the "gnashing of teeth" was clearly audible, and hence the imposture could be revealed and denounced immediately. Rushing toward the window that opened out onto the garden, the two priests found it closed by wooden shutters—probably new ones, since they lacked even the smallest crack.

13

THE BISHOP WHO BECAME A SAINT

lthough Don Pietro did not realize that he had been spied on, his failure to make peace with his colleagues led him to approach the archpriest of Dossena, the rural dean with jurisdiction over all of them, whose authority extended as far as the Valtellina, by now reduced to obedience to the Catholic faith. This may have been a preemptive strike designed to forestall a move by his adversaries. Nevertheless, the time had come for him to report the extraordinary fact about which he had had no doubt for more than a year. The elderly dean, feigning astonishment and interest, instructed Morali to continue giving communion to the exemplary daughter of the Church pending the forthcoming visit of the new bishop, to whom he would immediately convey the news.

Monsignor Gregorio Barbarigo had made his solemn entry into his diocese on 27 March 1658. Beginning his long pastoral visit in the mountainous part of the Bergamasco in September, he reached Zorzone on 7 October. Scion of a noble Venetian family and a favorite of Cardinal Chigi (the future Pope Alexander VII), Barbarigo had been named bishop at the age of thirty, a year after having taken holy orders. He is the only character in our story whose fame would outlive it—not, of course, because of his marginal involvement in it, but rather because of his expertise in theology and his particular devotion to the cause of clerical education. These activities would lead Clement XIII in the following century to beatify him. The good pope of our own day, John XXIII, judging it unfortunate that a bishop of his home town, Bergamo, had received no further recognition, would canonize him in 1960.

For us humble researchers reconstructing this story, it seems appropriate to stop the camera at the moment in which Maria of Vertova, who was straining at the leash to be proclaimed a living saint, encountered Barbarigo. That distinguished scholar and prelate, though he had good reason to expect that the red hat of a cardinal lay in his immediate future, could not of course have anticipated that in three conclaves he would come close to being elected pope, and he was even further from imagining that one day he would be promoted to sainthood.

No doubt the young woman from the mountains was awed by the title of bishop, an authority capable of recognizing or rejecting her heavenly privilege. Rarely has anyone been so completely at the mercy of another when nothing concrete was at stake. Her anxiety must have been shared by Don Pietro, who—though he bore the primary responsibility for the two, or rather the three, of them—could occupy himself with practical matters. He saw personally to the preparations for that historic day in the life of the village, making sure that the road was strewn with green branches, the church was adorned, the bells were tuned, and the refreshments were made ready (unfortunately the bishop would already have lunched in Serina), to the point of staying up till all hours and losing his voice. Maria, on the other hand, aside from the usual attention to her dress, which on anyone else's part would have been a less than venial sin, made ready only within herself.

The bishop arrived with his entourage in the afternoon, as Morali had calculated after pacing out the road from Oltre il Colle along the Parina creek, where the horses would stop to drink. Entering the church to conduct vespers, the bishop delivered a brief sermon to the faithful, who listened with devotion and rapt attention calculated to wound the vicar general—a carryover from the tenure of Bishop Grimani—against whom they had appealed in defense of their curate. Monsignor Barbarigo then blessed the baptismal font and visited the sacristy, the base of the adjoining bell tower, and the cemetery, located on a ledge projecting out between the houses. Then he went into the rectory to inspect the registers of births, deaths, and marriages. He put a few routine questions to the curate, who was impatient to tell him more important things. For the moment, however, Father Morali had to restrict himself to reporting that his stipend, to which all the families in the parish contributed, amounted to 560 lire a year for saying 160 masses, including those on feast days. No public sinners or people who refused to make confession were to be found in his parish. "There are no disorders," he stated, "and a small number of parishioners, all of whom obey me."

Now it was time for the refreshments, or rather the moment for introducing the distinguished visitor to the heads of the *contrade*,[1] and at long last to Maria. According to Don Pietro, whose account we have already heard in part, Bishop Barbarigo, having seen the young woman and been told about her gift of living on communion alone, "paused." Among those accompanying him was a Jesuit from the Visconti family; the two of them interrogated the woman and appeared to be satisfied with her responses. The bishop may have commented that "this must be verified."[2] He charged his vicar general with collecting written testimony from the curate. In addition, since he was not prepared to challenge or confirm on the spot such an extraordinary phenomenon—his reason for visiting Zorzone, which accorded with his personal inclination, was merely to dispense paternal smiles and exhortations—he delegated the Holy Office to look into the matter.

Morali's deposition, taken in another room of the rectory, was the first document from Bergamo to land on Fra Ambrogio's desk in Venice. Unbeknownst to the deponent, it was recorded in such a way as to constitute a basis for charges against him. Father Morali recognized his prime accuser, the vicar general, who had received the complaint from the rector of Vertova, but he was too impulsive to hold a grudge, and he put all his faith in the seemingly favorable disposition of the new bishop. Thus he found himself in the hands of a keen barber with a very sharp razor. But he had asked for the treatment.

Struck by the mechanical, sometimes brutal questions, he still did not recognize the trap, intent as he was on not missing the great opportunity to see all Maria's merits put down on paper. "In the morning she says her prayers, always concentrating on the mysteries of the most holy Rosary, and takes communion, after which she returns home. At noon she says her prayers again, then reads the lives of the saints and of the Virgin and other spiritual books, says the Office of the Blessed Virgin, and sometimes recites the Great Office, which I have taught her."

Hearing the account of such a thrilling life, which testifies more to good will and social mobility than to extraordinary gifts, any lis-

1. [Neighborhoods in the official sense, that is, administrative divisions of the village.]

2. ["Bisogna che questa cosa sia vera." As indicated in chapter 3, Morali, in reporting this statement to the Holy Office, chose to interpret it in a more positive light.]

tener, in addition to being bored, would become suspicious. Aside from the hour of mass and communion in the morning, the vicar general inquired, did this devout daughter of the Church ever go out of the house?

Her spokesman explained. "After church she doesn't leave the house except to go into a nearby meadow to read. This past summer she went to visit two sick people, who asked to be remembered in her prayers. She told them that they should put their trust in the Lord, for her prayers were worth little. And those sick people got better."

Paving the way with this unconvincing example, he was adroitly coming to the main point. Among all the other cures brought about by his pupil, he concentrated on the one performed on his sister, "abandoned by the doctors, having lost heart," the credibility of which he believed was guaranteed by the tie of blood. Only then did he begin to realize that the vicar general was still his enemy, and through association of ideas he brought forth an episode featuring Maria's younger sister, in which the holiness of his protégé stood out in reverse, as on an engraver's stone. "Last week her sister, whose name is Caterina, came to see her, bringing her some grapes. Maria later told me that when she saw the grapes, an idea came into her head that suggested to her 'Eat these grapes, they're good.' She ate three or four of them, but they tasted bitter, so she spit them out and threw the others at the demon, thus eschewing temptation. And then she told me that for two days she tasted bitterness in her mouth from having eaten those grapes."

Now the vicar general moved toward the crucial point which, leaving aside his personal feelings, he felt obliged to affront in his inquisitorial capacity. The deponent had stated that he gave the woman communion daily, and even twice in the same day. Did he have permission from his superiors to do so?

Don Pietro improvised, as we already know, fudging a bit on the timing and a great deal on the content of the advice and orders he had received. He had, he claimed, sought the opinion of the archpriest of Dossena, who had told him to continue giving the woman communion until the bishop's visit.

But what about before then? "For what length of time" had he administered the eucharist more than once a day to the woman without consulting his direct superior?

For nine or ten months, but without letting the people observe it.

The poor priest believed that he should move the colloquy to a higher plane. He recalled that one evening while Maria was still living in Colombo's cold, remote house, an angel and a crucifix had appeared before her. She had addressed them as if they were two wayfarers of whose intentions she was uncertain: "If you are good, stay here and keep warm, and don't go away."

The bishop and his entourage departed. Father Pietro had every reason to be pleased with himself, but also to wake up with a start in the middle of the night.

14

THE GOOD PRIESTS

s we shall see, the witnesses most dangerous to Maria were her neighbors and certain close relatives. Father Morali's prime adversaries remained his colleagues.

Interpreting correctly the result of the pastoral visit, the priests of the surrounding parishes came out into the open. Their version of the occurrences in Zorzone and their assessment of the protagonists thereof were for the most part diametrically opposed to the opinions expressed by the common people, there and elsewhere, so much so as to sound like another bell, rung by enemies with the advantage of being believed automatically by their superiors. Their consciences not only justified but reinforced their animosity. As far as they were concerned, when the true facts seemed unimportant, it was perfectly legitimate to build on them or recast them as they saw fit in order to make them appear damaging. By acknowledging some inconsequential merits in the man against whom they aimed, they lessened the risk of being unmasked or overcome with scruples for acting in bad faith.

According to Girolamo Carara, the curate of Serina, Don Morali was so ignorant, stupid, and "simple" that he could hardly read two lines of the catechism. Giuseppe Merloni, rector of Oltre il Colle, confirmed while slightly softening this judgment: "He was ignorant and simple-minded, but he was considered to be a good man." The chaplain of Valpiana, Giuseppe Valle, struck harder, calling Morali "an ignorant, simple-minded man who could hardly read mass . . . and rather greedy." Though he claimed not to want anything from the people he blessed, he took money on the sly. "The people, noticing that he didn't spend a cent on the church, even though it needed furniture and other things, murmured and said that they didn't know where that money had gone, and that if he had spent it as was intended, the church would have been made of gold. Someone should write a book about that priest."

The first priest averred that the people of Zorzone had certainly not been edified by the relationship which Don Pietro maintained with that so-called religious woman. They shut themselves in the rectory; she even helped him dress in the sacristy before he celebrated mass. As for her vaunted privilege, he had heard that she had eaten in Serina in the house of Caterina Ferosa, as her hostess could testify, and young Bonfantelli had been told by Maria herself that one day the Devil had beaten her. How did Don Pietro perform his cures? Here was a good example. Bernardino Carara's young son had a crippled arm, and Bernardino Valle's boy had broken his. Both were taken to Zorzone to be blessed, and people claimed that a miracle had occurred, "but the crippled boy remained crippled, and the other one's arm was still broken."

The chaplain of Valpiana had discovered how the miracles came about and the reason why Morali was reputed to be a saint, a seer, and a prophet. When women came to be cured, the priest sent them first to Maria, who questioned them about their problems and the causes of their illnesses and then ran to report everything to her master. This Maria certainly didn't look or act like a saint. She wore embroidered blouses and white gloves. She was attractive, with a pink and white complexion. When she heard a funny story or a joke, she laughed. The accusing priest, who held such an elevated conception of holiness, had obviously never aimed at it himself, since he went on to make fun of the good intentions of the most defenseless of the trio, Pietro Palazzi, who had also tried not to eat from one Thursday to the next in order to have visions and revelations, but on the eighth day "he ate everything." Finally, Don Morali gave the aspiring saint communion at times when the church was most crowded, and her attitude in receiving it was clearly hypocritical, since she comported herself with "a certain haughtiness."

Such judgments, accusations, and insinuations, credible and in some cases pitiful, narrow even further the horizon of that little world in the mountains and cast an unnecessarily harsh light on our protagonists. A good part of the aversion for Morali becomes understandable when one learns that the unbalanced, imprudent, and self-centered priest was continually sticking his nose into others' spheres of jurisdiction, as for instance when he dissuaded a man from Valpiana from ordering masses for his wife because he was certain that she was already in heaven, or when he bragged to one of his colleagues who was satisfied with normal piety that he had the power to force a storm to drop its torrent on a rocky mountaintop. In their view he was the classic braggart who lived by his wits, didn't keep his promises, ran up debts, and boasted about possessing qualities he lacked. Hence they could hardly wait to see him get his comeuppance.

Four years after the visit of Monsignor Barbarigo, who had been made a cardinal and was about to be summoned to the Vatican and transferred to the see of Padua, the interrogations conducted in the curia of Bergamo continued at a hectic pace. The confident assertions of these good priests were sharply contradicted by the less strident but still resolute testimony furnished by the inhabitants of Zorzone and the surrounding area. Struck again by the sharp divergence, we may ask ourselves whether it was solely a matter of different or contrary mentalities. We notice that the detractors of Don Pietro and Maria also tended to belittle the inhabitants of their world, just as the latter, testifying partly in support of the two, defended their own dignity. The bitterness that principally motivated these good priests was the disparagement, and self-disparagement, characteristic of those touched by a bit of culture and invested with a small amount of absolute authority who never attain inner peace or self-sufficiency. They blame their lack of the narrowness of their native environment, having lost forever its natural sense of proportion and its humble, fertile openness to self-doubt. For the priests, when it came down to it, the curate and his disciple were two losers who hadn't made it and never could have made it. For the people, on the other hand, Morali and Janis remained above all two good, honest, well-intentioned people.[1]

During the twelve years of Don Pietro's apostolate in Zorzone, Giovanni Domenico Colombo, a cautious man who liked to "leave the truth where it lies," had never heard anyone speak ill of him. As far as his pupil was concerned, "people said that this Maria was a good woman, and that she was learned."

According to the younger Giovanni Palazzi, "Many held her to be a holy woman. . . . He was doing very well in that curacy, and I don't know why he left it because no one chased him out. Everyone liked him; in fact, when they heard that he wanted to leave, they told

---

1. [The expression used here is *da bene,* which is virtually impossible to translate with a single word.]

him they would raise his salary. . . . He was considered a good, holy man. . . . As far as I'm concerned, he honestly knew what was good and preached it at the altar, and to my knowledge he carried out the duties of his office well. . . . He has property he inherited in Zambla, and as far as his behavior goes, I don't know and I've never heard that he scandalized anyone . . . In our house we had a good opinion of Maria."

The citizen of Zorzone who had had the most contact with Don Pietro was the elder Palazzi. "I've always known the priest to be a good man. He was curate of our church of the Holy Trinity in Zorzone, and he comported himself well, and he made us all devout, teaching us how to pray.[2]. . . One couldn't help loving him for his virtues, and I've eaten many times with him in his house. . . . All of us went there at one time or another . . . I've never seen him doing anything but good, and good works. Beyond that, I'm not accustomed to searching into higher things."

His daughter-in-law the innkeeper, Caterina Palazzi, spoke about the close relationship between the two. "I heard them talking about good things, and about the Lord. . . . I never heard anything bad against him, and I always thought well of him. . . . I considered him to be a good man, and other people did, too, and he ran his church well."

Margarita Castellina, rumored to be a witch, denied against her own interest what she had allegedly confided to one of the priests. "Of those who came to be blessed, some brought baskets of pears, others chestnuts, still others handkerchiefs, but he said, and I heard it, that they should give those things to the Virgin of the Belt because he was nothing, and if they were cured, it was the Madonna who cured them and not he." She had told someone, the witness was reminded, that when the priest left, he took with him a nice nest egg. "Good Lord," replied the sorceress, "I couldn't have said that because I don't know it, and if I knew it or had heard it, I would say so."

Don Pietro and Maria had sometimes gone to visit Caterina Fer-

2. That the witness meant this literally is confirmed by the statement of the young priest Don Giacomo Fadini Tiraboschi, assigned to Zorzone only twenty years before Don Morali began his ministry there: "When I went there to serve as chaplain, I found all those souls like so many lambs who had no idea of Christian Doctrine or other aspects of the faith." Quoted by P. Enrico Gino Ceroni, *Oltre il Colle: Una perla tra le Alpi Orobie* (Bologna: Grafiche Dehoniane for the Parrocchia di S. Bartolomeo di Oltre il Colle, 1979), 94.

osa, a young woman of twenty-five who had sporadically followed the informal rule of Zorzone. According to the rector of Serina, they had dined with her. "No, sir," Ferosa replied, "Donna Maria sat on one side of the table, but she didn't eat or drink anything." On that same day the two friends from Zorzone had allegedly blessed her clothes and given her a ring. "I know people said so, but it wasn't true, and I told those who were saying so that it wasn't true. . . . I think that the rumor came from the fact that I had just put on a religious habit, the one I'm still wearing, in order to feel better. . . . When I was in the house we sometimes joked around and put our mother's ring on our fingers, and it could be that someone saw us."

Giovanni Bonfantelli, a twenty-seven-year-old miller from Serina, had supposedly told the rector of Maria's confiding in him that she had been beaten by the Devil. "I never told him any such thing." Don Girolamo Carara in person had reported it. "That's just not true."

For a layman testifying under oath before the Holy Office, it took a good deal of courage to call his own parish priest a liar solely out of respect for the truth. On the other hand, the more the good priests launched accusations and raged, the more they were believed. They even described what they considered to be a conspiracy of silence on the part of the common people, making a summary prediction which reeks with disdain. "Those people in Zorzone and environs are crude mountain people, simple-minded and easy to fool. Hence they believed it to be true that that woman was a saint, that she didn't eat, that she had revelations, and all the other things the priest claimed. We priests in the vicinity didn't believe a word of it, but we had to keep quiet because the rabble adored him like a saint. They even said that as long as that priest was in the village, it wouldn't be struck by lightning."

The substance of the testimony and the opinions of the three priests, delivered when Don Pietro and Maria were in jail, had been known for the most part to the inquisitor in Bergamo even before the bishop's visit to Zorzone. After having absorbed the shock of the deposition transformed into an interrogation, Don Pietro confidently awaited a summons to the curia. Instead, as we have seen, he was called in by the inquisitor, still eager to bring him to trial and barely kept on the leash by Monsignor Barbarigo. The bishop's prudence no doubt attests to the nobility of his soul, but it also demonstrates once again that this was an era in which sainthood was achieved more through cautious and irreproachable behavior than through extraordinary gifts—and Maria had nothing to offer but miracles.

In his encounter with Fra Vincenzo Maria Rivali da Bologna, Don Pietro must have been subjected to a tongue-lashing which he would later try to minimize, although he admitted that the inquisitor had warned him to make sure that his protégé was a saint and not a devil. As we know, Father Pietro probably replied that all that was required was to conduct a test, at which point the friar very likely showed him the door.

From the point of view of our priest—whose father may have spoiled him by lashing out at and then forgetting his son's minor transgressions (or else have been relatively patient with the little boy, who may already have been disfigured by that noticeable scar on his forehead)—this was the sort of behavior to be expected from one's superiors. He was not prepared, however, for the letter that arrived before long from the bishop, in which he was ordered in no uncertain terms to send the woman back to her own home in Colzate. Seven years had passed since she had left there, and it seemed as if she had always lived in Zorzone. Hence, leaving aside the issue of her holiness, as far as Don Pietro was concerned, she was no longer Maria Janis of Vertova. Such an order would have been cruel if it had been intended to deprive a man of his beloved. In this case the woman was a perfectly innocent companion, and more than that, a source of inspiration for him.

Father Morali knew that he could not obey the command. The three intellectuals in Zorzone talked the matter over, consulting together and separately. Their reactions shifted from bitterness to protest, from indignation to rebellion. The passages in the Holy Scriptures concerning the tribulations of the just came to mind and then were set aside, since it would have been presumptuous, though all too easy, for them to identify their persecutors. Finally they decided that there had been a misunderstanding which sooner or later would be cleared up. Don Pietro was now clear in his mind that he need not obey.

Then he received a second letter from the bishop, punctual and identical like the notice of an unpaid bill. The three could only conclude that the world was large and the justice they were seeking was to be found elsewhere than in the diocese of Bergamo. Even without the complications that had arisen, they must have reasoned, their case could not be discussed, much less resolved, in a local forum designed to handle ordinary administrative matters. It required consideration by someone on high, the discretionary liberality of a powerful person. Had they needed to appeal a civil case, they would have looked toward Venice, but in their situation the alternative to Zorzone could only be Rome, the residence of God's representative on earth. Though Rome was far away, one could get there in stages, practically without noticing or remembering how long the trip had been, just as one might suddenly find oneself in paradise.

Don Pietro went down to the episcopal palace in Bergamo to make a legitimate request as a small recompense for the trouble he had undergone. Since Barbarigo, who had communicated with him through the vicar general, would not receive him, he left a message asking for a dimissory which would permit him to carry on his ministry outside the diocese. Once again, the prelate, in the spirit of a paternal shepherd of his flock, gained time by sticking to the letter of canon law: he had someone inform the priest that since he was a paid, removable curate, he would have to find a substitute. This requirement struck Morali as equivalent to the forced donation of a valuable asset, as well as a reminder of his own unworthiness. At this point, an unexpected encounter—one which from his point of view promised to pave the way toward the fulfillment of his and his followers' destiny and from ours gives the plot a new twist—served to mitigate his rancor and at the same time demonstrate that it was well founded.

15

THE RICH MAN PAYS A VISIT

$\mathcal{S}$ ome of the laymen who had accompanied Monsignor Barbarigo on his pastoral visit had been much impressed by Maria and the curate of Zorzone. Heading down from Oltre il Colle, the little cortege began to split up at Serina, grew even smaller at Sedrina, and more or less dissolved at Botta. This village lay beneath the palace of the Vitali, facing the last hill that blocked the view of Bergamo at the point where the Val Brembana intersects the valleys of Giongo and Imagna (the latter running all the way down from the foot of Mount Resegone near Lecco). No longer constrained by the standards of impeccable behavior required in the bishop's entourage, two friends of the Vitali family took the opportunity to spend a little more time in the countryside before returning to the city.

To the master of the villa, a young nobleman happy in his marriage but still without children—and worse, blind as a consequence of a hunting accident—they reported about that strange village, swarming with excited people, in which a holy woman and the curate were performing miracles. Count Agostino, a devout man if for no other reason than that his uncle Maffeo was Bishop of Mantua (but the family tree of the Vitali also included a cardinal and a friar who had been beatified), immediately picked up from his enthusiastic and affectionate friends the idea of making a pilgrimage to Zorzone. After some hesitation and a couple of postponements, in early December he ordered that his horse be saddled.

Accompanied by his servant Taddeo Vitali, the young nobleman arrived at dusk in the little town, which at this season was almost buried in yellowish slush. He found lodging in the improvised inn run by the Palazzi family, where Donna Caterina made him welcome and entertained him in the manner befitting the most distinguished guest who had ever come her way. Though she was impressed by his rich clothing and bearing, what struck her most was his blindness. Forgetting his title, she thought of him, and then began to refer to him when talking with others, as "Agostino the blind man." She guessed why he had come before she asked the reason and assured him privately that the priest would cure him with the help of a saintly woman she knew, who through prayer could achieve anything the gentleman might want, even reattaching a hand cut off his arm. No, she couldn't reveal who this angel of paradise was and where she might be found. The woman lived in retirement, supported by alms, and enjoyed a great privilege from heaven which must be kept secret for now but would eventually become public knowledge.

Yielding to his curiosity and assuming that here was one of those harmless extortions that the poor practice on spendthrift rich people, the young count searched in his purse and pulled out a large coin. The hostess thanked him on behalf of the woman, promising to give her the money right away. In exchange, the gentleman's prayer would be granted.

The next morning Vitali was received by the priest about whom he had heard such great things. Preoccupied with the urgent necessity of making contact with another bishop, Don Morali interrogated him about why he had come. The count replied that he wanted to recover his sight. How had he lost it? He had been shot in the face. Then he must have faith in God and in His Son Jesus Christ, Who in the Gospel had promised to grant the prayers of those who believed in Him. Did the gentleman believe? Yes, he believed. Then he should kneel, say three Our Fathers in honor of the Holy Trinity and a Hail Mary to the Virgin of the Belt. If he had faith, he would be cured.

The gentleman, accustomed to paying even for kindness, found this transaction so simple that for a moment he was gently transported back to the world of his childhood. Returning to adulthood, he felt as if he had been wrapped in fleece by a shepherd. Besides the matter of his sight, he mentioned, there was the problem of the children whom he and his wife had long but vainly awaited.

He'd come to the right place, the good priest's reassuring sigh seemed to suggest. Asking heaven for children was his specialty. He had brought happiness to a Brescian gentleman, a nobleman from Lodi, and many, many others who were still grateful to him. It was enough to have faith. The curate's voice must have sounded persuasive, for the rich pilgrim, who lacked the ability to study people's faces, received such a favorable impression that he returned home excited by the faith conveyed to him, for which the healer had not wanted a cent.

The two met again in the gentleman's palace one evening in January, probably just after the Christmas season. Signor Agostino was glad to have him there, despite the fact that "according to the righteous will of God" (as he piously put it when writing to his uncle the bishop), he still could not see him, and his wife—granted, it was a little too soon—had not yet announced any good news. Don Pietro was on his way to Bergamo, where he intended to try once again to talk with Monsignor Barbarigo about a matter close to his heart.

Count Vitali invited him to supper and offered him a bed for the night. At table the guest brought up the mysterious saint who lived in his parish, painting a picture of her even more stimulating than that sketched out earlier by the innkeeper. Although the master did not reveal the nature of his pupil's privilege, he assured his host that the woman had reached such a level of perfection that she was content to live in a basement room furnished only with a straw pallet. He asked the count to recommend her to the bishop so that she might be admitted to a convent or some other place of prayer. Monsignor himself during his pastoral visit, he claimed, had been edified by the young woman, and the Jesuit fathers, especially one who was a member of the Visconti family, had remarked that she should be held in great regard.

The next morning Father Pietro went on his way to Bergamo. That evening he returned to the villa. He reported to Signor Agostino that the bishop, who was about to leave for Venice, had told him only that "he could not attend to these matters." So depressed did the priest sound that this time it was his client who felt obliged to urge him to have faith. The count would not let his guest leave without accepting an offering for his impoverished holy woman. ("He gave him two gold coins, but whether they were *dobli* or *zecchini* I don't know," the alert Caterina Palazzi would later report.)

Now that a way out had presented itself, Don Pietro went looking for a colleague who might substitute for him, someone from elsewhere than the pleasant basin of Oltre il Colle, and he found him in Oneda, near Maria's native home. But the bishop, who insisted on being obeyed, responded to Morali's bitter message that he was prepared to give up everything and leave by informing him via the vicar general that if he wanted a dimissory, he had first to detach himself from the woman and send her home to her family.

In Zorzone they planned their escape. It took about a month to arrange all the details. They would leave in the dark of night so as not to disturb the poor villagers, who might try to stop them. But Don Pietro was incapable of keeping his mouth shut. He complained publicly about the malice and ingratitude of the world, lamented the fact that his decision was irrevocable, and predicted hard times for himself and his parishioners. Inferring that he wanted a change of air, the village notables offered him a higher salary. He had closed his accounts, he replied, and wanted only the balance due him and their friendship. In his Sunday sermon he wounded them with a terse farewell: "Goodbye forever. I want to wander through the world. I'll pray for you. Pray for me." Thus Morali had ruined the carefully conceived plan. To preserve some element of surprise, it was essential to reorganize themselves and leave before the faithful recovered from the shock.

During Don Pietro's tenure as curate, Zorzone had become accustomed to people thronging the narrow streets that ran between the walls of the houses and stables, but there had probably never been so many at night as the crowd that assembled in the church square at the moment of the "secret" flight. Gathered around the three runaways and the mule loaded with their baggage were the other three members of the Janis family, who had come up from Colzate, as well as Pietro Palazzi's half brother, sister-in-law, and old father. The elder Palazzi and Caterina had come to shed a tear and then go back to bed. Maria's mother, too, headed back down the road toward home carrying two bulky sacks containing belongings that might not be of any use to her but should not under any circumstances be left to others. For Margarita Castellina, bundled up against the cold in order to peer out her dark window, this last was the juiciest detail.

The young ones were leaving, and God go with them, since everything happens according to His will. After climbing up to Oltre il Colle, the three fugitives, accompanied by the younger Giovanni Palazzi and Maria's siblings, headed down the road toward Serina. They were not the sort to turn back to bid farewell to the faint line of their native mountains. The cold of the February night and the crunch of their footsteps on the frozen mud heightened their sense of insignificance, thus putting to the test the audacious dream that had led them to challenge it. "Until we meet again, forever."[1] Pronounced from the pulpit by Don Pietro, theirs was the farewell of emigrants who cannot express themselves very well and choose to leave in part for that very reason. Perhaps only the versifier Palazzi, who was born in the Zorzone basin and had never ventured beyond it, felt some pang of regret. But the only woman he had ever loved, wearing stout men's boots, was preceding him down the road, and he followed her like a dog whose entire satisfaction comes from being faithful.

They arrived in Botta before the sun rose. Awakened by the servants, Signor Agostino, as soon as he recognized the pilgrims, assigned them an apartment, considering himself "most favored by the privilege of lodging these servants of God."

The sun also rose in Zorzone, bringing to light evidence of the flight that no one had really believed would occur. Wandering around the square, the church, and the rectory, the villagers seemed to be looking at a big empty nest that was still warm. They felt the shock of a departure that seemed to have been motivated by spite. What had happened was so important and so obvious that it defied common sense and reawakened old prejudices. Snatches of conversations overheard behind doors gave rise to the wildest conjectures. They'd gone to Loreto to visit the Holy House. No, to Rome, summoned by the Pope. Someone went so far as to whisper the name of the most holy and distant city in this world, on the doorstep of paradise: Jerusalem, a word that fills and purifies the mouth. Finally, the conjectures gave way to the more straightforward and mundane consensus that the curate had done wrong to leave by night with a pretty young woman.

1. ["A rivedersi per sempre"; the correct, logical form would be "addio per sempre."]

16

THE BEGINNING OF A
JOURNEY

*O*n a journey undertaken by the poor, for whom the world opens at the edge of their village, most of the surprises, difficulties, and satisfactions come at the very beginning, partly because at that point their senses are more highly attuned.

Father Pietro called a halt at the villa of the affable Vitali in order to take a rest after a winter night on the road. First of all, he asked to say mass. Then he explained their intention to go to the Holy House at Loreto and hinted at the urgent necessity of finding a bishop from whom to obtain his dimissory letter. The master of the house readily offered to recommend the good priest to his uncle, the bishop of Mantua, and was prepared to do even more. Since he himself had to go to Mantua the next week, he would accompany them. In the meantime, while waiting for him, they could make themselves at home in the palace, occupied only by himself, his young wife, the servants, and his old aunt Caterina, the bishop's sister, who never left her apartment. The villa also had its own chapel. Few gentlemen, in the count's opinion, had the privilege of playing host to a priest held to be a saint and a mysterious woman reputed to be even more saintly, whom he finally had the opportunity to meet.

His curiosity and satisfaction were returned. Maria, who had taken a look at the private chapel, was certainly not displeased, especially since she was encouraged to invite her sister to stay with her. For the first time in her life, Caterina Janis would sleep in a bed with a headboard, thus attaining the social prestige and the associated comfort already enjoyed by her sister. No one asked Palazzi's opinion. Since Don Pietro was the guide and director of the little group, he had also assumed responsibility for their expenses. From now on, from his point of view, every day passed as someone else's guests would be a day gained. Maria's and Palazzi's brothers, having completed their escort duties, headed back together and then parted, each returning to his own home.

In assigning rooms, the proprietors of the villa were guided by the criteria of decency and respect commensurate with their relatively modest resources. The two Pietros were put up in a room on the second floor, the two sisters in another higher up. Thus Maria, who had lived so long in huts and basement rooms, began an exciting new phase of her career upstairs.

As far as meals were concerned, the group's spiritual father had to reveal to their hosts certain things which in a house like theirs could hardly remain secret. Signor Agostino and Signora Paola, as well as being people of the world, were a pious couple. Once they had recovered from the shock, they informed the servants about the special status of their oddly attired female guest, whose polite reserve discouraged jokes and gossip about her, at least outside the precincts of the villa. It was decided that Caterina would be served her meals in the room the sisters shared, so that she could keep Maria company and because her presence at table with a priest would be inappropriate. She was to be fed abundantly, however. After all, she was a healthy, robust girl of twenty.

Their life in the villa was not tightly scheduled. The first thing in the morning Father Pietro said mass in the little chapel connected to the palace. In the evenings he devoted himself to raising the spirits of the childless couple. He did not hesitate to describe in detail the rare privilege possessed by his pupil, declaring himself certain "that people would see great signs and miracles descend from heaven on Maria." Signor Agostino thought he merited a preview: what signs? But the priest, tracing a circle with his finger, limited himself to whispering, "A ring . . . ," and let them draw their own conclusions.[1]

The visitors and their hosts, however, did not devote themselves exclusively to spiritual matters. Morning mass was often sung, which in villages happened only on Sundays. They lunched and dined in the great hall, and in the evenings Maria came down and took part in the conversation by the fireside. For the four guests from Colzate and Zorzone, the stay with the Vitali was the first vacation of their lives. Caterina took the fullest advantage of it. She wandered around the

1. [Agostino and Paola Vitali would have understood that Morali was alluding to a forthcoming mystical marriage between Maria and Christ.]

palace, discovering one thing after another. She went into the kitchen to chat with the cook. On the sheltered loggia, attached almost like a piece of lace to the facade of the palace, which overlooked the little river Giongo, she even tried her hand at shaving the priest. And how she ate, stimulating her appetite and aiding her digestion with excellent wine!

Caterina's meals were served by Antonia Trionfino, about the same age as her mother but with the keen eye and memory of an experienced servant. Every noon Antonia carried up a jug of wine and "about twelve ounces"[2] of bread. "If we were eating meat, I served them a nice piece, sometimes roasted and sometimes boiled, about twelve or fourteen ounces of meat. I took them a nice big bowl of soup and a good hunk of cheese, which Signora Paola cut off for me. And on meatless days I gave them *casoncelli*,[3] omelettes, and other things, depending on what the cook prepared, but always a good amount sufficient for both of them, that is, for Maria and Caterina. When I went to clear the table, sometimes there was something left, but not much, and other times nothing. Whatever was not eaten I sometimes left there rather than taking it away, and when I returned to clear the table, everything was gone."

Antonia's description of these meals, which were undoubtedly prepared with a care and culinary skill now almost lost, is enough to whet our appetites, especially after so much discussion of fasting. Although she was able to sniff the aroma, Maria seems to have been above such things. She may even have taken pleasure in seeing her sister appease her lifelong hunger, a hunger which she herself managed to suffocate.

As we have heard, though both bread and meat were served in abundance, the pieces of meat outweighed the chunks of bread. The servant, however, made it clear that Caterina was free to go into a "little room" adjacent to Antonia's where the entire store of bread for the household was kept. When this wasn't enough, nothing prevented her from helping herself in the larder. On occasion she came down-

---

2. [The Bergamasque *oncia* was equivalent to 27.094 grams. *Tavole di ragguaglio dei pesi e delle misure già in uso nelle varie provincie del Regno col sistema metrico decimale* (Rome: Stamperia Reale, 1877), 108. The modern Anglo-American ounce is slightly larger: 28.34953 grams.]

3. Ravioli filled with cheese.

stairs to ask for food, saying she was hungry, and took it up to her room.

The days passed happily, and the house guests even received visitors. Mother Janis took to the road again to check in on her daughters, concerned particularly for the younger, who was still in her charge. The elder Palazzi, who had in Botta a son, a friend who was a priest, and a former tenant, came along with her. He was a garrulous old fellow whom everyone liked. A trundle bed for Mamma Lucrezia (whose elegant first name only the count could recall later) was put into her daughters' room, and there was no skimping on meals. Having spent the weekend at the villa, the two parents departed, much relieved and refreshed.

The happiest of all was Signor Agostino, who was not yet thirty. Since it was Carnival time and it was raining, he saw no reason for their hurrying away. He put off his departure for Mantua, where he planned on "enjoying himself for two or three months" in his uncle's palace. The prospect of such a long vacation heightened his good humor. He played the guitar, which in his blindness was a great comfort, and on the last evening of Carnival they danced in the Janis sisters' room. Antonia Trionfino had to admit that she had not seen them dance, but she "certainly heard the noise, and when I asked the other servant, Maria della Botta, and Signora Paola what had gone on to make so much noise, they told me that they were having a good time."

The young countess had developed an affection for Maria that resembled a crush. After blessing two shirts, one belonging to the countess and the other to her husband, and advising Signora Paola to keep them, Maria had then traced the sign of the cross on three candles, telling her that in case of bad weather she should light them all at once "and it won't storm at all." The countess, having first consulted her husband, asked the religious woman to bless all the rooms in the palace. In exchange she smartened up her guest's appearance, first giving her a crimson skirt made of fine cloth, then having a new black dress made for her, which Maria wore drawn in at the waist by "a leather belt like those of St. Augustine."

Although, as her husband later admitted, Paola Vitali did not believe in Maria's divine privilege, the young gentlewoman became so close to her guest that she even saw to her coiffure. Antonia testified that "she did her hair, braiding it, as I once saw, and they used the mirror." Though she went into the women visitors' room without knocking, the assiduous and omnipresent servant never surprised the guest eating or drinking. Once she saw the aspiring saint in her underwear. "She was dressed underneath like a man, with cloth underpants that appeared to be black, and she wore a man's jacket. I know because I saw her one morning in her room when I went there to take her something, a comb or something else, I don't remember. I saw Maria without that black dress she usually wore. She was seated in a chair, dressed like a man, as I've said, and Signora Paola was doing her hair."

Curious but not particularly disturbed about what she had observed, the servant asked her mistress why in the world the woman dressed so peculiarly even underneath. The lady of the house replied, "So that she can ride better." Not even the inquisitor of Bergamo paid much attention to these details when, three years later, he finally had to give up trying to interrogate the young countess, who was always ill. He was, however, interested in determining whether the wanderer's clothes might not be sacrilegious—whether her stole, for example, was embroidered with the sign of the cross. Antonia Trionfino told him that all she had seen of the stole was its fringe.

In addition to the servants, who did not express themselves openly, there was another person in the villa who didn't like the guests, particularly not Maria. Aunt Caterina, a spinster, spent the long winter days in her apartment, which she never left even to attend mass in the nearby chapel. Perhaps she was so feeble that the most she could do was sit on a cushion at her window to get a look at the strange people her nephew had dragged into the house. She heard a great deal about them from the servants, who, unable to express themselves freely in the presence of their master and mistress, allowed themselves to blow off a little steam in her apartment. Thus, counting the hours between cups of clear broth and measured rations of boiled meat, she probably learned of the uninterrupted fast allegedly undertaken by the secluded visitor. Only in God did Maria have a less visible and more assiduous supervisor, and He was on her side. Unwilling to admit that she might be mistaken, the old lady bitterly observed in a servant's presence (and her remark would later be accepted as credible testimony),[4] "She said she didn't eat, but she ate more than all the rest." And when she heard

4. [By the time of the trial Caterina Vitali was dead.]

that at long last the horses were being saddled for the guests' departure, her comment was "Yes, they're going to Rome to be canonized." Either Maria realized that she was being watched, or else her relationship with the lady of the house had deteriorated. She grew nervous and impatient to proceed on, or better, to begin, the great journey. For too long, she, who didn't allow herself anything but the daily communion wafer, had let herself be drawn into the recreation and frivolity of the others. She may have asked herself whether they had left Zorzone merely to find a new place in which to pass their time.

One evening—the hours long after communion were always the most difficult for her—she broke down in sobs. Pietro Palazzi, called in the villa her guardian angel, who had enlivened Signor Agostino's afternoons by "improvising verses," had to go downstairs and interrupt their master: Maria was crying and wanted to see him. The priest left the company and went up to console her.

Therefore their host decided that it was time to depart. Vitali, who did not want to be outdone in courtesy by his wife, had given their most honored guest a cloak made to measure for her in the villa. After the celebration of mass and the usual communion, Don Pietro and Palazzi mounted two rented horses sent up from Bergamo. Maria climbed onto the mule, grown lazy in the well-furnished stall, and the blind gentleman rode his war horse alongside his servitor Andrea Algherati. Sulking Caterina was left behind. As they rode along, the servant, distantly related to the count and older than Morali, felt obliged to give the curate a piece of advice: they should go back to their village. It was exactly the stimulus Don Pietro needed right then. Since it came from a person of his own social status, this counsel was obviously wrong.

Accompanied by a gentleman named Bonavolo and two members of the Capeletto family, who would go with them as far as Mantua, the party arrived around noon at Palazzolo sull'Oglio, where they stopped for lunch. At the inn, Maria, who did not sit down at table, urged them to hurry because the food with its earthy odor was making her nauseous—we should not forget that she had been riding on an empty stomach—and was compelled to go outside. Pietro Palazzi immediately finished his meal and ran out to join her. Since their departure from Zorzone, and especially during this stage of the journey, the two had been whispering to each other. Having taken a big piece of bread from the table, Palazzi explained to the others later that he had given it to the mule. Signor Agostino and his servitor Algherati made nothing of it. From their point of view, Maria during this journey satisfied all the needs of an ordinary woman, as her healthy appearance showed, and the former weaver Pietro had come along to take care of her.

They decided to stay overnight at Ospitaletto, just west of Brescia. Palazzi chose the inn and a room for Maria, who retired immediately and stayed there. Early the next morning they found a church for mass and communion, much needed at that point. This was the first time that Morali had to celebrate mass outside his diocese, for which he needed a dimissory. The parish priest, like an inattentive customs officer, didn't ask him for it, and Don Pietro was not concerned, since for him the license with a signature and seal was required only by ecclesiastical regulations, not by God.

From Ospitaletto they headed for Montichiari, where, since it was Lent, they limited themselves to the midday meal. This time Maria, whose hunger and thirst had been appeased, stayed for awhile by the fireplace. In the warm, well-stocked inn, Signor Agostino, who could already smell the air of Mantua, lifted the wine flask toward the only woman in the group, inviting her to help herself, and he did the same with the platters of food, well chosen and abundant. "But she made fun of it, laughing."

At dawn it was her turn to eat, but that morning what was bound to happen eventually took place. The rector of Montichiari, with the key to the sacristy in his hand, asked Don Pietro for his dimissory. The only alternative was to go on to the next church. Maria's face was as pale as a rag.

When the sun was already up, they reached Guidizzolo. The priest in this little town, not a man to stand on ceremony, was proud to do a favor to a colleague in such distinguished company. Maria's face regained its color. Now they pressed on to Mantua, stopping briefly at Goito to take a little refreshment. Here one of Maria's few false moves attracted attention and fueled the servitor Algherati's suspicion. As she helped to clear the table, she took a piece of bread and moved away from the group.

On the outskirts of Mantua Count Agostino was recognized as

a close relative of the bishop. He dictated to a man named Simone a letter to his uncle requesting that rooms be prepared for his guests, a holy woman and an equally worthy priest, accompanied by their servant. Algherati was charged with delivering it. Either this bishop had the sixth sense of a vigilant pastor or he had already heard about the trio from the Bergamasco. The moment he read the letter, "he got angry and said that he certainly did not want to lodge them, and that his nephew shouldn't go around with that sort of people."

Algherati returned to the group, who could read the bishop's reply on his face. Embarrassed, Signor Agostino hastily directed the three to the Sun Inn, where the two Capelettos and Bonavolo also took rooms, and went off to confront his uncle Maffeo. Even before putting his bags in the room assigned to him, he went into the bishop's study to fulfill his promise. The moment he heard the word dimissory, the uncle "flew into a rage, gave me a good dressing down, and sent one of his minions to tell Father Morali and the woman that they had better make tracks out of the Duchy of Mantua. Because it was evening, the city gates were already locked, so the priest and the woman stayed overnight in the inn."

Even more short-tempered than strict, the bishop was not satisfied. Having learned that the city gates had already been closed, he summoned Algherati, ordering him to go at dawn to awaken the three and tell them in his name "that they must get out of the city and its territory." In executing his commission, the envoy gave the pious trio from the mountains what was probably the rudest awakening of their lives. "They were frightened and weeping. I told them to go back home, but they said they wanted to go to Rome. Therefore I accompanied them to the Ferrara gate. They had a little mule with them."

The tears of the pilgrims, once again fugitives, did not move Algherati, who because of his distant kinship with the family was not exactly a servant, though he did not rank as a gentleman. He demanded back the valise lent them by his master, forcing the curate to dump his possessions into a sack. He later remarked, "When I saw that instead of having patience and relying on God, they fell into despair, I was scandalized, and I said to myself that if they were saints, as they claimed, they would have turned to God and trusted in Him." For us, on the contrary, it is at this furthest remove from their aspirations that they achieve their fullest humanity.

But the rich can be human, too. Indeed, rich gentlemen frequently show themselves truer to their word than members of the lower classes, who are often constrained to play tricks at others' expense in order to attain a legitimate objective or get themselves out of trouble. In the face of pressure from his uncle, Agostino Vitali did not bow his head or abandon his convictions. The bishop, wary, perhaps because he had come out on the short end of some business transaction, and harsh with the defenseless because he was generous with himself and obsequious toward his superiors, wrote a servile letter to the inquisitor of his diocese reporting on what had happened and the measures he had taken. Probably hoping to elicit another accusation enhanced by a partial admission of responsibility, he forced his nephew to do the same. The young blind gentleman, however, dictated an account of what he knew and had observed, adding his own opinion. "On the journey I received nothing but edification from both of them in conversation, both on the road and when we stopped at inns. . . . In addition, let me assure you that everyone thought very well of them, as their manner of life merited."

The count maintained contact by letter with his friend the curate, who wrote shortly after their happy arrival in Rome, where, he said, he had had no difficulty obtaining the dimissory letter. As a matter of fact, the priest was telling one of his not infrequent and unnecessary lies, presumably with the intention of comforting Vitali for the rebuff received from his uncle, rather than to have him pass the word to the bishop that in the Eternal City there were bishops on intimate terms with the pope who were much more charitable than he.[5] In addition, Don Pietro gave further proof of his own credulity in reporting that when he had forgotten his purse with all his savings on the table in an inn, a peasant had run after him to return it, and he sent greetings from the *religiosa* Maria.

Wait a moment: had he written "the *religiosa*[6] Maria" or "the angelic virgin Maria?," asked the inquisitor of Bergamo, for whom all mortal sins either stemmed from fornication or verged on sacrilege.

---

5. It is impossible to share the opinion of the compilers of a book about Botta who call Monsignor Maffeo Vitali a man of "exemplary charity." *Noi di Botta ieri e oggi nel 40° di consecrazione della chiesa parrocchiale,* ed. P. Ferdinando Cortinovis (Botta di Sedrina: Comunità parrocchiale di Botta di Sedrina, 1976), 32.

6. [See chapter 5, note 2.]

Fra Vincenzo Maria put this question to the servant Taddeo, who had read the letter to its recipient. Even at the apex of the Baroque age, the servant who had accompanied Signor Agostino to Zorzone did not place excessive weight on adjectives. He remembered that in one letter the greetings came from the "angelic" Maria, but as to the title reserved for a very different Maria, "I don't recall that he used the term 'virgin,' although he often gave her the name 'the *religiosa* Maria.'"

17

MARIA'S FAMILY

*T*hree years after their last contact with Maria, the Janis family also appeared before the inquisitor of Bergamo, Fra Vincenzo Maria. They did not show as much care as Signor Agostino in defending the two fugitives who had fallen into the hands of the judicial authorities. Lucrezia Janis would have staked her life on the fact that her daughter did not eat, at least in her presence, after moving into the Palazzi household, where the mother had gone to visit, sometimes staying for three days. In responding to the last question, however, she fell into a trap. On the night Maria departed, hadn't the daughter, who had been richly repaid for the so-called graces she performed for the sick, given the mother two sacks filled with valuable items to take back home? The old peasant woman—forced at an early age to play a woman's role, only to become a child again when she reached old age—tried to make things clear, just as our mothers and grandmothers do today, using exactly the same words. "She took the good and beautiful things with her and left the rags for me."

Giovanni Battista Janis, the son and brother, had never seen Maria eat when he had gone to visit her in the basement room in Zorzone. He never stayed more than an hour or so, however, because he had to get back to his work in Zambla.

For what reason, the inquisitor asked him, had his sister taken up with the two men?

"I don't know, sir. I believe it was because of her affection for the priest and for Pietro Palazzi."

The testimony furnished by Maria's sister Caterina, whom we already know, deserves closer attention. She did not slip into the inquisitor's usual well-disguised traps. Instead, without being asked, she pushed her sister into one with both hands.

In the cellar of the Palazzi house, where Maria had kept the bread and cheeses people gave her, the young woman had stuffed her belly well, just as she did later at the Vitali villa. But Maria herself had taken advantage of the provisions twice or three times, "maybe more or less." Returning one day to the cellar room, the younger sister had caught Maria "with something in her mouth. I don't know what it was, but it was something to eat, and she put it in her mouth and chewed. If she kept eating or gave up eating later I don't know, because I didn't see her."

Thus, at the very end of the long and thus far fruitless examination of witnesses, the Holy Office obtained from a relative, who was therefore above suspicion, a proof of Maria's pretense which shook the entire edifice of the so-called heavenly privilege to its foundations. The district inquisitor believed that what he called "the knot of eating" was finally on the point of being untied. All he needed to do was lead the witness, who was more than willing to collaborate, in the right direction by asking her in a confidential manner whether her sister had ever eaten with her when they were in the Palazzi household.

Fra Vincenzo Maria scored, as his superior Fra Ambrogio had not yet managed to do. "Once she and I ate a milk soup I had made, other times she ate on her own. I know this because, in addition to having seen her eat as I've just said, she was given bread and other things by the people there, and although she sometimes gave bread to the children, there was always food there, and she could have eaten it if she wanted, even though she told me that she didn't eat. Anyway, when I was with my sister in the Palazzi house, I went upstairs to Giovanni Palazzi's kitchen to cook—barley soup, gnocchi, polenta,[1] and other things—and then I took them down to the room where my sister was, and there I ate them. Sometimes there were leftovers, which I left in the room, and when I came back, I noticed that there was less food—not always, but sometimes. As far as I recall, she never ate with me except that time when she ate that milk soup."

This line of questioning, which had seemed so promising, hadn't in fact yielded very much. The inquisitor, unable to hide his disappointment, began to threaten her before he became really angry. If Caterina's sister had eaten once in her company, that meant that Maria

---

1. [Gnocchi: potato dumplings; polenta: cornmeal mush, served hot (as in this case) or allowed to cool, sliced, and fried.]

trusted her and hence nourished herself regularly like everyone else in this world. Therefore the witness should be careful not to give false testimony, for in effect she was lying to God.

"I'm telling the truth. I don't remember that in the Palazzi house she ate with me except when we ate that soup."

The inquisitor had already examined all the servants from the Vitali villa, where Caterina had been in intimate contact with her sister for two weeks. If what he had been told thus far was true, Caterina's appetite had appeared to be insatiable.

Showing the same indifference with which she had just got her sister in trouble, the young woman admitted that she was a glutton. "There in Botta in Signor Agostino's palace they put the two of us in a room upstairs, where they brought us our food. A servant in the house brought it. I ate, but I never saw Maria eat."

Never had Maria been more exposed to temptation but in better control of herself than during those two weeks of vacation. Whether at that time she succeeded completely in maintaining her fast, or rather managed to eat on the sly without being observed by her sister, who now had more reason to confess than to conceal the truth, we are compelled to admire her performance. When she returned to the stand in Venice, however, she would have to defend herself against the obstinacy of Fra Ambrogio Fracassini, who, although he had the authority to absolve her of much greater sins, believed that he finally had his hands on a half-truth of minor importance. Now he wanted the whole truth at all costs.

III
THE FORCED CAPITULATION

18

THE DEVIL'S ROAD

*F*ra Ambrogio Fracassini, inquisitor general of the Venetian Republic, had read the transcripts of the interrogations conducted in Bergamo. On long, thin sheets of paper he had copied out the most incriminating phrases, thereby preserving for us what could be mistaken for the notebook of an amateur poet. Or to put it in another way, perhaps we can say that as opposed to exaggerated claims of severity, the evidence of giving in to earthly appetites which commonly goes under the name of sin is in itself material for poetry. The vocabulary of the trial records, which in typical seventeenth-century fashion followed an identical trajectory, confirms this impression: the lower it went, the more it interested the prosecutor, who marked passages concerning the appetites with one or two crosses. Compared to the saint's lives written by Maria's companions, disconnected and extemporaneous, the transcripts, thus annotated, reveal an entirely different taste and mental orientation. Here are a few examples. "She was eighteen, pretty, plump, pink and white, a lovely, lovable girl." "She often went to the priest's house during the day, and she could have gone there at night, too." "Passing by one evening around dusk, after the Ave Maria had sounded . . . I could hear the gnashing of teeth, and Pietro Palazzi was there because I recognized his voice." "He took her to a room upstairs and stayed there with the door closed, explaining later that he was engaged in mental prayer."

Our female protagonist had languished in prison for almost five months when, on 27 June, she was called to make her third appearance in the chapel of San Teodoro. We can imagine her "worn out and thin," as in Colombo's barn, because eating, even prison rations, was not good for her. But Fra Ambrogio, bent over his notes, paid attention only to what he heard, and Maria had to help herself out by staging a little scene for which she had had ample time to prepare herself.

Asked whether she was ready to confess that she had eaten, as the testimony of many witnesses made clear, the defendant ran through in her mind the people from the mountains who had gone down in groups from the two valleys and converged on the inquisitor's headquarters in Bergamo Alta. Not knowing who had said what, she had to find a response that would either refute them all or corroborate the testimony in her favor. "It isn't true that I've eaten!," she exclaimed. Then she abruptly broke off, suddenly taken ill. "I think I'm going to faint," she murmured. "The same thing happened when I got out of bed this morning, but even though I'm not well, I came here in order to obey."

When no one gave her a hand or sustained her with a sympathetic glance, she took hold of herself and went on. She had always told the truth and would continue to do so. She had not eaten, and if anyone had said otherwise, that was his problem. Or perhaps, having seen her pretend to eat, someone had thought that she was really eating. "Since I'm half stunned, I don't fully understand what you're saying, although as far as eating is concerned, I'm telling the truth that I didn't eat, and I know what I'm saying."

Before confronting her with the most decisive testimony against her, the inquisitor cited the report from Calle della Stua about the pasta sprinkled with cheese and the act of putting food to her mouth revealed by Pietro Palazzi's half brother, the sausage-maker in Cannaregio.

In no place had she eaten.

Because the long period of imprisonment had done nothing to make the defendant cooperative, it was necessary for Fra Ambrogio to lay down his trump card, the testimony of her sister. The steam of the milk soup, the polenta, and the gnocchi which Caterina had cooked over the Palazzi fireplace and carried up to dish out before the enraptured but familiar gaze of her elder sister rose again in the chapel of San Teodoro. Maria had fully trusted in her sister's discretion and loyalty. Now she passed a damning judgment on her. "If that's what my sister claimed, she's an idiot who doesn't know what she's saying, because I didn't eat."

The inquisitor now fudged a little by attributing to Caterina Janis the more detailed testimony of the observant domestic in the villa at Botta about the leftovers which had disappeared from the plate.

Not getting the response he wanted, he enumerated the dishes served, named Antonia Trionfino, exorcised the ghost of Count Vitali's malicious old aunt, and recalled the journey with stops at the inns in Goito and Guidizzolo, where both she and Pietro Palazzi had taken bread away from the table.

At this point, either forced to invent some means of defending herself or sincerely convinced that the truth was on her side, Maria no longer drew any distinction between servants and masters. "All those witnesses who claim that I ate are false, and I'm telling the truth." Since she did not suspect that the two passers-by who had stopped under the window of Morali's house and heard "the gnashing of teeth" were priests, she included them among the prevaricators. "Those who say that I ate are all liars."

What had become of all the loaves of bread and the cheeses she kept in her cellar room, and from whom had she received them?

They were given to her in charity, and she had distributed them to the poor.

People gave her food, knowing that she didn't eat?

With almost mocking lucidity, Maria parried the blow. They gave her food because they knew that it would be passed on in new acts of charity.

The inquisitor struck back by attempting to damage her self-esteem. How everyone had made fun of her privilege! And she, in order to publicize it better, made fun of those whom she saw eating, saying that they were eating dirt and filth, while she alone was nourished by spiritual bread.

Janis felt the blow. "Filth" was her word for excrement.[1] She tried to recover by becoming theatrical again in order to show that she was sick and tired of sparring over a question that obviously meant a great deal to her. "Loudly and emphatically" she burst out, "A curse on eating!" Then she stopped, recognizing the need to clarify the matter for the reverend fathers on the tribunal, who took food at least twice a day. "For me, I mean, not for others, because my health has deteriorated now that I have to eat."

She had reached for a high note and had not missed. Their silence seemed to indicate consent, which she sought to make sure of

1. *Sporchezze*. Even today, when dogs and cats empty their bowels, well-mannered peasants say that they are "dirtying" (*sporcano*).

by trying again for a low-key exit line that would evoke applause. "I don't say that I'm holy, but I'm so glad to be free of the nuisance of eating that I laugh for joy." Still, her mark on the transcript, which had earlier been so large and firm, now tilted to one side like the wooden crosses in old country cemeteries.

Since as far as eating was concerned, the defendant showed no sign of yielding and the transcripts from Bergamo had not proven particularly useful, Fra Ambrogio decided that it would be better to follow the lead of Fra Vincenzo Maria Rivali. When he learned during the interrogation of Caterina Palazzi that Maria might have been bewitched, the inquisitor of Bergamo, thinking that he had his hands on something important that could shed light on her fast, had promptly called it to the intention of "my most reverend father." By the time he interrogated Janis again on 11 July, the Venetian inquisitor was also considering the possibility that she had had relations with the Devil, who had taken possession of her to such an extent that he inspired her every thought and action. If put in this perspective, as regulated by the Devil, the absurd, contradictory universe of Maria might fall into place, becoming coherent and concrete. It almost seemed as if the obsessively observant Catholic from Vertova were about to be transported back more than a century and treated like one of the many witches tried in those Alpine valleys in the early sixteenth century.[2] Oddly enough, from the transcripts it appears that she herself was the first person to utter the word "witch," the term she used in reference to her first hostess in Zorzone, Margarita Castellina. What in fact was the relationship between the two women: secret complicity or acrimonious opposition?

Before the tribunal of the Inquisition the holy woman and the "witch" found themselves allied. Castellina had thought it wise not to defame such a pious woman, and Maria now realized that it was not

2. [Recent research has made abundantly clear that inquisitors in Italy, Spain, and Portugal preceded their lay and clerical counterparts in northern Europe and North America by at least half a century in becoming skeptical about the reality of witchcraft and diabolical possession and hence relatively lenient in their treatment of alleged witches. See, for example, Giovanni Romeo, *Inquisitori, esorcisti e streghe nell'Italia della Controriforma* (Florence: Sansoni, 1990).]

appropriate either to arrogate to herself the role of judge or to lower herself by becoming an informer. She replied that she had applied the term to the old woman because everyone in the village considered Margarita a witch, and from the old woman's attitude and behavior one could infer that she "did not have a pure heart." That was all she had intended to imply.

The Devil was capable of predicting the future, the inquisitor observed—to know in advance, for instance, that the weaver Palazzi would not be "drafted into the service of the Prince." [3]

Maria did not remember this incident. Her retiring into her room, concentrating, and returning to her hosts with the good news "Don't worry, there's nothing to be afraid of," however, was characteristic of her. "That [I said such a thing] could be," the defendant admitted.

The Devil knew everything about the status of people who had passed into the next world, even poor anonymous folk mowed down by the plague who had ended up in purgatory.

This time Maria remembered. Kneeling in prayer, she had been informed that those souls were still expiating their sins.

Among the occult powers of the Evil One were causing and deflecting storms.

Yes, she had first said the Our Father and the Hail Mary. Then she had taken a hailstone, crushed it, and thrown it on the ground. The hail had stopped, but by virtue of the prayers directed to God and His Holy Mother.

And what about the sorcery of lighting three candles at one time?

In this case she was paying honor to the Most Holy Trinity.

So as to subject her completely and use her to his best advantage, the Evil One had taught her the magical art of healing the sick.

Of all the cures she had performed, Maria remembered most vividly the assistance given her by Heaven in helping her master's sister, "who didn't eat anything but an egg a day." After the prayer and the benediction, "I gave her two eggs, which she ate. She continued to eat and got so much better that she was able to get out of bed."

Was it true, then, that this woman from the mountains knew

3. The doge of Venice was called a "prince" (in the sense of "ruler") even though his position was elective.

how to read Latin?[4] The inquisitor handed her the Roman Breviary
and asked her to read. She passed the test: "Debiliter sed tamen hon-
este legit [she read with difficulty but correctly]."

The Devil's profane project included suggesting that she put on
the white stole and the habit, but under her garments she wore men's
clothing. According to the *Malleus maleficarum,* she must have done so
"in honor of the goddess Venus."[5]

"I've always dressed as a woman, but on trips I wore trousers
underneath for convenience in riding and to protect myself from the
cold."

And on that evening of Carnival at the villa in Botta, hadn't she
betrayed her mania for dancing?

"Never in my life have I danced. It's true that Signor Agostino
played the guitar, but I didn't see anyone dancing."

The Enemy's main purpose for her was to seduce the curate and
pursue with him an ever more iniquitous enterprise directed against
God. Hadn't she even gone into the sacristy on the pretext of helping
him to put on his vestments?

This was not true. In church she either knelt at the confessional
when she intended to make her confession or, if she needed to talk
with the priest about something else, she went up to ask him and then
returned to her pew.

But she had gone to see him in his house, where she cooked for
him, and they stayed in a room together with the door closed, claiming
that they were engaged in mental prayer.

She had never cooked for the curate, nor had she stayed in a
room alone with him.

But here in Venice she did the cooking, and at the end they were
living together day and night!

4. [According to the current paradigm of witchcraft, possessed persons who knew
only their own vernaculars might utter words in Latin or Greek put into their mouths
by the Devil.]

5. In his introduction to the modern Italian translation of the famous witchcraft
manual, Armando Verdiglione cites the account included in the Dominican friar Jo-
hannes Nider's *Formicarium* (1435–37) of "a girl who dressed in men's clothing, even
though she declared herself a woman and a virgin. After long hesitation over the
diabolical or divine character of the phenomenon, the authorities burned her." *Il mar-
tello delle streghe,* trans. Fabrizio Buia, Elena Caetani, Renato Castelli, Valeria La Via,
Franco Mori, and Ettore Percella (Venice: Marsilio, 1977), 24.

In Venice they stayed in other people's houses, but in Zorzone they lived in their separate homes.

Even there, however, they were alone together. The priest went to see her in her basement room and didn't let others set foot in it.

They always saw each other in the company of Pietro Palazzi.

The inquisitor pushed the hypothesis of a diabolically inspired conspiracy one step further. Palazzi, he asserted, had also been caught in the seductress's net. The three of them were so intimate "that people said they were all in love with each other."

Maria was not taken aback. She knew that she had avoided and redirected the weaver's love, the better to spiritualize her own love for Don Pietro. "We were on close terms not for evil purposes but only to serve God, and our affection for each other was entirely centered on God."

In the apartment in Calle della Stua, where they had been arrested, the priest went so far as to help her make her bed and warm it.

That wasn't true.

The trustworthy person who had so testified was able to pinpoint the time it happened as between eight and nine in the evening.

That was completely false.

In that same room, before giving her communion, hadn't the priest tied a white band around her head?

She herself had put on the scarf.

From the testimony of witnesses, on the contrary, it was clear that it was Don Morali who had arranged and tied the head covering.

Not so. Never had the priest touched her head.

The inquisitor had neglected to confirm with Antonia Bellini what she had told her confessor about the moment of intimacy between her two neighbors. (She had twice seen the woman touch the priest—"I don't know whether reverently or affectionately, once putting her hand on his shoulder, another time resting her head on his shoulder.") Strangely, he abbreviated the episode and shifted the action from Maria to Morali, thus failing to make explicit use of one of the very few pieces of evidence about the defendant's possible involvement in a love affair. It almost seems as if he thought that amidst so many other charges, a touching moment of romantic intimacy might serve to validate her innocence. Aware that from this point of view the behavior of the two appeared almost irreproachable, he chose to employ it indirectly in order to augment their guilt, to show them—he would soon use the same approach with Don Pietro—how much their other misdeeds had put them at risk of committing sexual sins. On 20 July he reminded her that she had actually carried consecrated hosts between her breasts, thus committing sacrilege by daring to transform one of the most sexually charged parts of the female body into a tabernacle. But that wasn't all. Why had she let Father Morali take out the box containing the wafers, "putting his hand in your breast, with manifest danger of sin on both your parts? Why did you, who made so much of your holiness and goodness, not take it out yourself?"

In the transcript the word "sin" is abbreviated,[6] not out of prudery but rather out of laziness on the part of the chancellor, who was accustomed to having to take down the term all too often in such proceedings (though in fact in this case he had to do so only twice). Transmitted to us in this form, the word conveys the intensity with which it was pronounced and the impact it must have had on the defendant, reinforced by the inquisitor's paternal disdain and regret for such behavior on the part of one who claimed to be so holy and good. Sacrilege, a crime committed by perverse people, was Fra Ambrogio's business in his role of inquisitor. Carnal sin, on the other hand, concerned him as a friar confessor: it deprived a man (not to mention a woman) of the right to be called good, excluding him or her from the select group of those who had taken the vow of chastity. Hence the friar, innocent of sexual experience, was particularly afraid of it. It is tempting to imagine Fra Ambrogio, in the act of confessing an ordinary female penitent, accentuating his expression of regret for the sin with deliberate physical contact between them, such as squeezing her finger or touching his burning forehead to hers.

Maria, who hadn't sinned in this way, did not seem particularly disturbed. On the contrary, leaving aside the unintentional comic element imposed by the situation, she showed a respect even greater than Morali's for her body, worthy of housing the sacrament, as well as for the wafers themselves, which her unconsecrated hands were not permitted to touch. In any event, she minimized the inclination of her spiritual father and life companion toward physical contact. "When

6. [*Pec.*, standing for *peccato.*].

my master wanted to give me communion, I with due reverence took [the box] from my breast by pulling up the green cord, and when it was out of my breast he took it, and then he put it back, returning it to my breast."

During these three sessions, Maria sensed that her long fast, against which there was no conclusive counter-evidence, was the strongest point in her favor. As she put it on 27 June, whoever wanted to believe in her privilege could do so, "and whoever doesn't can leave it alone." It almost seems as if she knew that the transcripts from Bergamo contained a practically identical statement by the elder Palazzi, one of some thirty witnesses who had not seen her eat but the only one who conceded that she might have. "However that may be, I don't know how she lived. God can do anything."

For his part, the inquisitor let it be known that although he had spent more time and effort on this case than was usual in such proceedings, he had still not got very far. According to the rules of the Holy Office, however, he could not proceed to judgment without having obtained a confession. Hence, during the interrogation on 20 July, he declared his resolve to get her to confess with the means prescribed for recalcitrant defendants, that is, "with the torments of torture."

Maria had read many saints' lives. The best she could hope for from the high court, which refused to believe her despite her demonstrated willingness to collaborate, was martyrdom. "I've told the truth, and if I'm tortured, I'll remain firm."

In this as in all other cases, the inquisitor functioned as attorney for God. After the threat, which had not produced the desired result, he decided to travel the Devil's road to the end by pushing the hypothesis of an evil plan to its ultimate conclusion. If Maria had been possessed while she was fasting, she could not have received the angels' bread; in that case, her so-called celestial privilege was instead an infernal prerogative. Hence the theologian needed to ascertain whether she had fallen into the Devil's clutches before or after having begun her fast.

Right at the beginning, she replied, while she was living in Colombo's house and when she went home for her father's funeral.

Was she eating at that time?

Janis affirmed explicitly that rather than having yielded to the Devil, she had been conquered by her appetite. "I had eaten and drunk, and for that reason I went home not wishing to observe my privilege." And with earthy candor that suggests to us that renunciation was not always pleasant, she added, "Of course, since I didn't want to continue living on communion alone, I had to eat."

Why had she gone home to eat and drink when she could have done so in Zorzone?

She had returned because it seemed better to eat and drink with her own people than before strangers. Thus we can infer that this was an interruption rather than a renunciation of her fast, a tactic adopted to force Don Pietro to pay more attention to her and implemented in Colzate so as not to ruin her credit in Zorzone. The curate, as we know, came to see her and was disappointed. She let herself be exorcised so that he would believe in her privilege once and for all.

This, however, is obviously not the explanation the defendant offered. On the contrary, to conceal her real motives, she attributed so much initiative to the Devil that she put him in the service of God. The Evil One had attacked her because instead of nourishing herself on the bread of the angels, she had gone back to living on that of men.

Watching Maria fall into this enormous error, the inquisitor let her dig herself deeper and deeper into the hole. Then he observed that the Devil should have been delighted when she resumed eating and should have tormented her when she claimed to be enjoying the heavenly privilege. All this, therefore, was her own invention, or if she preferred, a diabolical illusion.

Before replying, Maria "remained silent for some time [cum multum cogitasset]." She realized that the inquisitor had trapped her and that what he maintained was correct, but she still was not convinced that she was wrong, for if she were, the reverend father would have told her so earlier. Her position was completely consistent with the popular conception of divinity, semi-pagan and Manichaean, which she did nothing but articulate, albeit in particularly vivid terms. The Devil, the complete impersonation of evil, represented the negative side of God, Who in His complete goodness could not act evilly. Therefore He subcontracted negative assignments to His mortal

enemy, expert in evildoing, who thus became God's chastiser or exe-
cutioner. It was Satan who had hinted to her that the bread consecrated in Calle della Stua might not be the real sacrament, who appeared to her with a crown on his head to deny that in the box at her
breast she was holding the King of the Universe. Was the Devil not
therefore serving the interests of God and the Church? Had Fra Ambrogio been shrewder or less sure of himself, he would have become
really angry. From the defendant's clouded perspective, he himself was
consistently performing the Devil's functions, or to put it in another
way, the Devil was Heaven's grand inquisitor.

Maria limited herself to recognizing that she had been defeated
on the grounds of logic, not that she had been unmasked. She reiterated feebly, "I've told the truth."

Her accuser accepted this as the beginning of her surrender. He
declared that she was "vehemently suspect on the grounds of the witnesses' testimony and practically convicted by her own words." Following the required formula, he asked whether she believed that the
witnesses had been examined properly.

She thought that they had been but reserved the right to explain
herself further and raise objections at the proper time.

Did she intend to mount a defense?

If she were assigned one or two attorneys, she would consider
doing so.

By this time her mark on the transcript had become a minus-
cule x.

Six days later, in the heat of late
July, she asked that the captain who had arrested her take her back
before the Holy Office. The inquisitor granted her request, sure of a
confession that would lessen her guilt and save him the trouble of
having her tortured. As it happened, he became a spectator in a scene
of the drama not included in the script. At that very moment, however, Maria's theatrical talent slipped away from her.

Captain Michielini, on loan from the secular government with a
miserable salary and therefore symbolically compensated in the trial
transcript with the recurrent adjective "valiant," accompanied her to

the judges' bench. The inquisitor asked her to confirm "whether she had petitioned through the captain to be brought back and heard again by this tribunal, and to say what she had in mind."

Maria had just one thing to say, which she had already repeated a hundred times. Instead of the new development the judges expected, her only recourse was a different sort of comportment. Should she be more forceful or more compliant? Was having shown the courage to ask to be heard again in an extraordinary session of the tribunal an asset, or would it be perceived as an affront? Precisely because her monologue was not theatrical, it was the testing ground for a true actress, who at this point had to cease being one.

"It's true that I made the request, and I'm here to say what I need to say. It's been approximately five years that I've neither eaten nor drunk—more than that, as I've heard in the parts of the trial record which were read to me, which confirm the truth of what I'm saying now. It's about five years since I've neither eaten nor drunk, and before that, for about a year, there were the trials of going for eight, fifteen, twenty days without food. After that, I stopped eating entirely."

It didn't work. They still didn't believe her. The judges remained unresponsive, at the most curious, as if they were watching a scene that was going better than before and might end in an unexpected way. Maria caved in. "I feel my heart being suffocated. I think I'm about to faint. I need to rest a while."

Unfortunately the bench for those being interrogated had been removed from the room. Having said that she needed to rest, she had no alternative but to sit down on the floor in an awkward and perhaps immodest way. The only sound in the room was the scratching of the chancellor's pen as he took down her last words, her gestures, and now her silence.

Suddenly she arose, exclaiming "Take heed! You don't believe the truth, only the lies!"

The chancellor wrote that down and summarized what followed. "Et post haec siluit, per dimidiam partem quarti horae. Et cum nihil aliud praeter nugas diceret, fuit remissa ad Carceres. [After that, she was silent for half a quarter-hour. And having said nothing but nonsense, she was sent back to prison.]"

Those seven and a half minutes of silence constitute perhaps the first recorded sit-in in a courtroom, conducted by a woman who was asking both so little and so much. With them Maria's divine adventure concluded. Now nothing remained for her but to finish traveling her human course.

19

THE MAD PROPOSAL

On 26 July Father Pietro Morali came back into the courtroom after four months in prison. During this time his conviction about the faith imparted by God in exchange for absolute faith in the promises of the Gospel had deepened. In addition, he pinned his hopes on the manuscript describing the main tenets of the extemporized rule followed at Zorzone, which was in the hands of the Holy Office.

This fuzzy and argumentative treatise, to which the inquisitor did not pay much attention, can be summarized in terms that are already familiar to us. He had consecrated the host and celebrated communion in a private house following a direct suggestion from the Virgin, who had assured Maria that she need not be deprived of her celestial sustenance: "My Son permits your master to consecrate the host by using only the words of consecration of the bread." He had acted in obedience to this divine directive. He knew that he had done the right thing, since otherwise he would have felt repugnance.

Once again Fra Ambrogio objected that Holy Mother Church, directed by the Holy Spirit, had ordered that consecration not take place outside of a church, without an altar and vestments.

How was it possible, the curate inquired, that he was in error when his conscience was clear?

The inquisitor should have told him that his feeling was the sort of blind faith in a higher cause that justifies any action. It had made him violate a sacrament; it makes us break two of the commandments, "Love your neighbor" and "Do not kill." Instead, the accuser let him partially off the hook, telling him more or less that the Devil, who had inspired him and whom he had obeyed, had rewarded him by exempting him from feeling remorse. With this *ad hominem* argument the inquisitor scored, just as he had done with Maria.

For a good Catholic, and particularly for a Catholic priest, even one as inept as Don Pietro, the journey toward God is almost always a return via repentance. The renewed relationship is signaled by the keen chagrin of reconciliation. After a long period of confident and even bold service during which, thanks to the rich harvest he was reaping, he had never asked himself whether he was still in God's good graces, perhaps the curate from the mountains was suddenly called to account by his true Superior. Strangely enough, in His presence he sensed an unexpected and not unpleasant shadow of guilt—nothing more than a flash that, given the desolate circumstances in which he found himself, felt like a rough paternal caress. His awareness of this ethereal presence moving inside him may well have led him to the point of admitting, "It's certainly true that, with God's help, if I had it to do over again, I'd think harder and seek advice."

The inquisitor moved right onto the ground the priest had yielded. "The defendant is advised by this Holy Office to believe that these so-called revelations of his are either diabolical tricks and illusions or dreams and fictions of his own, and therefore he must tell us what he believes now."

Denying that they were his inventions, Don Morali began thinking out loud. "What should I say, that I have done right or wrong? On the basis of the explanations and admonitions furnished by this Holy Office, I must admit that what I have done [consecrating and administering communion outside of a church] has been done through diabolical illusion, and thus I retract and withdraw my opinion and humble myself in obedience to Holy Church and the Holy Office."

To all intents and purposes the curate of Zorzone had abdicated his priestly function, recognizing how badly he had performed it, but only in order to buttress his role as the unimpeachable prime witness, so as to rehabilitate himself through the merits of Maria. (She, in fact, might have renounced her privilege had she been able to put on a genuine consecrated stole.)[1] But in the eyes of the Holy Office, he remained a priest, however flawed. Now that he had admitted what seemed to his accusers to be his major crime, he would surely confess to the infractions and lies linked to it.

On 8 August, therefore, the inquisitor launched a barrage of accusations and insinuations in descending order of gravity, beginning

1. [That is, to function as a priest.]

with the intimate relationship with his pupil, designed to make Morali yield on the most controversial point, Maria's alleged fast. In Venice he had put his hands into her breast. He had warmed her bed. He had lived with her "in home and hearth," just as during their journeys and previous sojourns. In Zorzone they had closed themselves in rooms in both their houses and she had followed him into the sacristy, causing people to murmur. Someone had maintained that he had taken her away from Vertova when she was eighteen or twenty years old and "pretty, plump."

Answering point by point, Don Pietro persuades us, at least, of his lack of physical interest in his companion by a comment that we would not have expected from him. It wasn't true that Maria was pretty, "for she had a goiter which then disappeared after she began fasting."

He had looked her over, then, with a masculine eye and, not finding her to his liking, he had decided to remember that he was a priest and concern himself only with her soul. The young woman from Colzate, who had correctly interpreted the expression on his face, began to assign greater importance to the goiter (not infrequent among people in the mountains owing to lack of iodine) than it really had or than she would otherwise have admitted. Could a woman undertake a fast in the hope of eliminating or at least reducing a physical imperfection? Supported by good fortune, Maria managed to achieve two mutually exclusive ends: she further beautified her spirit, so that the priest would be forever enamored of it, and she rid herself of her bodily flaw, becoming first ugly and worn out, then beautiful, plump, holy, and free of the goiter.

For Don Pietro, who had limited himself to following her prodigious spiritual growth, she now became "a perfect woman in Our Lord God." The allure of her attractive appearance, which had perhaps emerged too late, may have been sublimated by the priest in the form of considerate, humane treatment. "Sometimes I warmed her bed when she was ill, behaving toward her like a father or mother in performing this service, and then I left to go about my own business. But I never made her bed or helped her make it."

This last suggestion, made by the inquisitor without any solid evidence, had been rejected also by Maria, who with equal firmness had denied that he had warmed her bed. To the curate's credit we can perhaps infer that he, ten years or so her senior, had used the bed-warmer when she wasn't watching, behaving tenderly like a parent—which almost makes us forget his ungentlemanly allusion to her goiter.

Fra Ambrogio then began to do some accounting. The business of the Confraternity of the Belt and the miracle cures must have been lucrative, as Don Pietro's supporting three people for five full years attested. Besides, some of his favors were paid back in hard cash by the affluent people with whom he had been shrewd enough to strike up an acquaintance.

With his accustomed zeal, Father Morali came clean and cooperated. It was true, he had received five *dobli* as a gift from the Duke of Modena and four *zecchini* from Signor Agostino Vitali to give to Maria. (Caterina Palazzi had mentioned two gold coins.) The proceeds from the sale of the belts, at fourteen *soldi* each, were spent on the poor. Before leaving, he had collected his stipend for a year and a half, amounting to eight hundred *lire,* to which he added sixty from his savings. For the mule, sold in Rome, he got fifteen Roman *scudi.* Even with all this money, they could hardly make ends meet, since they had to give alms to the needy, buy Maria's dresses, and save the unhappy Annamaria Casolina, who was prepared to die of hunger rather than offend God "when she was sought after by men who offered her money."

To this the inquisitor had no rebuttal. Then he fired at close range—or, if we prefer, let drop as if it had never been discussed before—the question of "whether Maria ate before she was imprisoned."

Don Pietro felt himself back on his home ground. "For about five years Maria has not eaten or drunk, nor have I ever seen her eat or drink, although to put up a good front and keep her secret, she has sometimes pretended to eat."

His adversary adduced proofs and clues in three distinct periods of time, which he presented, however, in an order inversely proportional to their weight. First, in Calle della Stua, under Maria's mattress and on the beams, the agents had found the headcheese and salami which the defendant and Pietro Palazzi had claimed to have put there with their own hands.

Palazzi, the curate replied, had brought them for him, and he had then hidden them in two safe places.

He was lying, since on the day after their arrest, the weaver had gone back to the apartment and looked under the mattress and on the beams without finding the food, which by then had been sequestered.

They both knew where the food was hidden, Morali responded.

The inquisitor passed to the second phase. The defendant had already been read the deposition which put him in the same room of the house in Venice where Maria was eating. He had replied that she had only been pretending to eat. Again, he must explain what had induced Maria Janis to pretend if no one else was present and could have seen her.

Once again Morali cited the five-year total fast, punctuated with an occasional legitimate simulation of eating.

Fra Ambrogio then turned to the third and earliest period of time. In Zorzone Father Pietro was in a position to give her food, either by going into her cellar room unobserved or passing it through the window. Furthermore, he could easily feed her day and night in his own house, which the woman visited freely, even shutting herself in a room upstairs and cooking for him and others. As a matter of fact, "one evening, passing by at dusk, after the Ave Maria had sounded . . .": he too was read the testimony of the two priests who listened under his window to the gnashing of teeth.

All lies and calumnies, he replied. He had left behind "some malicious persecutors in the village, who have falsely invented this lie." But who were those two mysterious passers-by who knew so well the layout of his house? Morali suddenly suspected that he had been betrayed by his most intimate friends, perhaps by the Palazzi, resentful about Pietro's departure and now sunk so low as to tattle about and twist friendly remarks and matters discussed in confidence. Overcome by a flood of bitterness and disappointment, he now saw the village as having turned completely against him. "I can say that they all hated me out of malice and envy."

The inquisitor took full advantage of Morali's moment of despair. He should take courage. Just as he had admitted that in consecrating and administering communion outside of church he had been deluded by the Devil, now he should make up his mind to confess that Maria's pretended sanctity was nothing but an invention of theirs designed "to fool the world so that they could live as they wished," and that the woman actually ate just like everyone else.

The mere mention of eating, without question the verb most frequently conjugated during this trial, was enough to revive Morali and make him dig in his heels like a mule. On every other issue he was ready to place himself "completely in the most loving arms and favors of the Holy Office," but not on Maria's privilege, for which he did not hesitate to mortgage even eternal life. "Since I must tell the truth as if I were on the point of death, never in my presence has she eaten. And it cannot be otherwise because she has always obeyed me, nor have I had any suspicion of her disobeying me."

After having dug carefully around the root of the lie hour after hour, the inquisitor realized that it was still firmly implanted. He was ready to rend his garments in frustration and rage. On 17 August he admonished Morali that although the witnesses had sworn to tell the truth, putting their souls on the line, the defendant persisted in denying it, despite all the evidence to the contrary. But "that which he was unwilling to confess under favorable circumstances, he would have to confess under rigorous treatment."

Like Maria, Don Pietro accepted the challenge and turned it against his antagonist. "I can tell nothing but the truth and what I know for certain. And if I am tortured and say the contrary, it will be against my will because of the torment, and I will have been forced to commit a mortal sin."

By touching his nerves, the threat had restored his determination, but then he too was disarmed by a wave of bitterness and solitude. He believed that he had been doing good, nor would he have acted as he did if he had believed otherwise; he would rather have died. "In the future," however, "with God's help, I will no longer do what I have done because it is no longer God's will that I do so."

Although the inquisitor might have considered this a new and more definitive surrender and guided it to a suitable conclusion, his expectations had been disappointed too many times. Unable to believe that the defendant had ceded, he indicated that he wanted to conclude the proceedings. Hence he asked the required questions. Did the witness have any doubts about the conduct of the two investigations and of the witnesses' good faith? Did he wish them to be reexamined?

Don Pietro accepted the proceedings of both tribunals and did not demand that the witnesses be questioned again. He could defend himself against the depositions of the witnesses heard in Bergamo, where everyone wished him ill, beginning with the priests envious of Maria's privilege, who from what he had heard, "wanted to have her so as to guide her on her road."

Did he intend to entrust his case to an attorney?

Into the priest's overwrought mind, pushed to the limit of physical and moral resistance and offered the opportunity to make the most of the last few minutes remaining to him to plead his cause before the entry of a lay lawyer extraneous to the case, came an idea so compelling and feasible that it took hold of him like the proposition of a bribe. He was obligated on pain of mortal sin to make known the truth about their voyage under God's guidance. Therefore he asked, in lieu of the defense to which he was entitled, "that an immediate test be made of Maria's new celestial privilege ... And I beg this Holy Tribunal that for the love of God, it begin right away, tomorrow or the day after, because I am the one who knows this sure and certain truth that Maria has the privilege of living on communion alone, and I am obligated to make this truth known to the best of my ability. The way to do so is this. If you do not want to leave her in prison where she is now, put her in some secure and honorable place above suspicion and have her well taken care of, as befits such a person, by trustworthy and God-fearing attendants. And there let her be given her celestial supper every day without fail for eight days if that's long enough, and if it isn't, for ten, twelve, or fifteen days in a row. After that, when the truth has become evident, Maria will be set free, as will I, her master, because this privilege bears with it the complete truth of our entire voyage. In this way the malice of the Devil and the world will be laid to rest."

The lost priest had more than revived: he was refilled with fervor and exaltation. He had no need of lawyers in robes and wigs. The test he proposed, which could be carried out immediately, was on a supernatural level. If he had not had arrayed against him the Devil and certain witnesses who had paraded before the two tribunals, then no one would have doubted Maria Janis's privilege and his word. "For my lawyer I choose this Holy Office, whose responsibility it is to ascertain the truth of this fact. And I'll give you my opinion about how this test should be conducted, which is that the Most Illustrious Monsignor Patriarch should take charge of it, along with the rest of you."

Who knows whether any of those present and directly solicited to accept the mad proposal gave Morali a commiserating glance as he was led back to prison? It is certain that the founding fathers of the Inquisition would never have foreseen a time when judges and defendant would be on such familiar terms that an invitation to collaborate would come from the accused. And if they had, they would not have welcomed it.

20

THE THIRD MAN GOES TO PRISON

Much to the regret of the Holy Office, Pietro Palazzi remained the principal witness, the one who had observed almost all of the defendants' incriminating behavior. Since he had been their constant companion, he was so inextricably linked to them that the inquisitor had not believed a thing he said. Even though the agents of the tribunal had not actually apprehended him making sacrilegious use of consecrated things, it is surprising that he had not been jailed with the others. The moment the door closed behind the pathetic curate, however, the members of the tribunal decided to summon him. Six days later, on 23 August, Palazzi appeared before them.

Fra Ambrogio had ready for him the array of questions and insinuations already put repeatedly and more and more forcefully to the two main architects of the rule of Zorzone. Only the complete understanding spontaneously reached by the three on the basis of shared principles and an identical way of life allows us to exclude the possibility that they had agreed in advance on the story they would present if they ran into trouble, or that each had some inside source of information about the interrogations undergone by the others. Thus, when asked whether Maria, when she arrived in Zorzone, had any distinguishing physical mark, Pietro confirmed that she had a goiter, but in his view "it did not make her deformed because it was small."

As we have seen, the inquisitor had managed to trap the woman on the issue of the chronology, and particularly the motives, of the Devil's intrusion into her life. The priest, however, had come off well on this score, asserting that the Devil had intervened to oppose, not encourage, the resumption of her fast. What did Pietro Palazzi think about all this?

Maria, he replied, had been possessed and then beaten by the Devil at the beginning of her total fast because the master of hell could not tolerate her living on communion alone. The witness had seen the physical signs of the beatings: the woman had appeared "so worn out and battered that she resembled a statue." No doubt he had in mind one of the many statues dripping blood which in that era competed to disturb the consciences of the faithful, and which Maria in a moment of severe pain may actually have wished to resemble.

Did the woman cook in the priest's house?

They both cooked, taking turns. After the food was on the table, Maria—who, it will be recalled, had denied preparing meals—withdrew from the kitchen.

At long last, after months of monotonous, inconclusive interrogation, the inquisitor, face to face with a man of the world who had been Maria's constant companion, could go beyond inquiring about the food the woman had consumed. He asked the witness whether "he had seen her give signs of having eaten and drunk."

Pietro Palazzi responded precisely. He had not seen her eat nor "give other natural signs as do those who eat and drink, not even during the journeys."

Beyond his faith in the special grace bestowed on the parishioner with whom he had shared lodgings for more than two years, the priest Morali, in his closing speech six days earlier, had assured the tribunal that he had certain evidence that his pupil had maintained a perfect, total fast. "I am the one who knows this certain, indisputable truth . . . and I am obligated to do everything I can to demonstrate it." Modesty, perhaps, along with the fear of appearing to have had even more intimate relations with the woman than the inquisitor had suggested, had kept him from being explicit. He had been liberal, even prodigal, in adducing proofs of a spiritual kind obtained in the confessional, and not a one of them had been accepted. What, then, could be the final, indisputable proof, as crude as it might seem, that would win acceptance from those who insisted on hard facts?

There is good reason to think that in Don Pietro's view, Maria would easily have passed even the test administered by St. Philip Neri. On the point of being convinced by an abbess that one of the lay sisters in her convent was maintaining a total fast, Saint Philip suddenly drew the mother superior aside and asked her with paternal solicitude, "Does this daughter move her bowels regularly?" The abbess, as if to defend the complete normality of her convent, hastened to reply, "But of course, Father."

Taken by itself, this subject verges on the comic. Nevertheless, even if one accepts completely the argument that Maria was pretending, it is worth considering for a moment the innumerable and not insignificant inconveniences which the woman from Vertova had been able to surmount, not only while living with others but especially when traveling with strangers and stopping at inns, where she had to control herself in order not to ruin her plan. At what point did it become easier not to eat at all? Furthermore, this line of reasoning, as the inquisitor seemed to suggest, while it increased the amount of favorable evidence in the possession of the two Pietros, aggravated their position by enhancing their role as her accomplices.

Fra Ambrogio, however, was in a position to fight back. In previous interrogations the witness had admitted that he had taken salami into the woman's room but had claimed they were for the priest. If that were the case, he would have hidden them under the priest's mattress.

Palazzi's response was identical to Morali's. He had hidden them for himself and the priest in Maria's bedroom because other people who might have taken them came into the rooms downstairs.

Since the curate had also assumed responsibility for hiding the salami, the inquisitor observed, one of the two was lying. But he decided to change the subject. According to witnesses, both in Count Agostino Vitali's palace and in various inns during the journey, the witness had suddenly got up from the table and left the room.

He had gone out to see whether the mule had been fed.

Or rather to help Maria eat on the sly, unobserved even by her sister? As a matter of fact, "when lodging in the homes of cultivated and noble people, it wasn't necessary or polite to get up from the table to check on the mule, who would have been fed by the servants."

It wasn't true that he had gone out to find Maria, who while they were in Botta had not been feeling well.

At the inns in Goito and Guidizzolo, hadn't he picked up an entire loaf of bread to give to the woman, who had also taken bread from the table?

Yes, both he and Maria had taken bread, but in order to give it to the mule.

Fra Ambrogio had certainly traveled to the outlying branches of the Holy Office, spending the night at inns at the crossroads, and thus he had considerable experience with innkeepers' hospitality. "Inns, particularly those on that road, are well provided with grain, the proper fodder for pack animals . . . and besides, their travel expenses were being paid by Signor Agostino Vitali."

Their mule, accustomed to the pastures in Zorzone, didn't like the grain and hay stocked for the horses who traveled that road.

Once again the inquisitor switched to another line of questioning. Given the fact that he was in possession of much more serious proof, such as the pasta sprinkled with cheese, to which Maria could have helped herself freely, it seems strange that he assigned such importance to the report about the gnashing of teeth, which had led him nowhere in his interrogation of the defendants. Of course the father prosecutor was obliged to believe the testimony of the two priests who had paused under the window to listen to the sounds of knives, forks, and jaws, but does Fra Ambrogio's insistence on this fragment of evidence betray his lack of trust in the two loquacious Venetian girls? What other evidence against Maria's fast did he have besides the impossibility of a human being's living for years and years without nutriment? The bowl of milk soup cooked by her closest relative, the one most anxious first to support her and then to betray her?

Pietro Palazzi did not hesitate to impugn the veracity of the two priests and the other inhabitants of Zorzone. "No one there was a friend of Father Morali because he admonished them."

For just a moment the friar laid aside his inquisitor's robe and donned the habit of a father preacher accustomed to sprinkling his sermons with aphorisms and metaphors. "When a pastor reproaches people and provides them a good example, they are not his enemies. On the contrary, they love him."

The weaver and assistant sausage-maker, who was both the most worldly and the most reactionary of the trio, took it upon himself to bring the friar up to date. "These days," he sighed, "there are people who don't want to be corrected." For this mistaken pedagogical effort he received his due reward. The Dominican did not appreciate being corrected so severely and rudely by a person who was at the very least suspect in matters of faith. Resuming his role of inquisitor, he retorted, "The Holy Office sees that the witness does not want to confess and state what really happened. Therefore he is paternally exhorted to confess and speak the truth, because if he does not, he will be shut up in prison and castigated severely, and furthermore he will be tortured to extort the truth from him."

Still afire with holy wrath, Palazzi could respond to such a threat only by raising his voice. He too saw himself faced with a sort of martyrdom. "Let the court do with me whatever it likes—torture me, roast me alive—for I cannot tell any other truth than what I have already said."

Such hyperbole betrays the specious indignation of one serving the common cause who knows that he has protectors elsewhere (and higher). It also resembles the kicking and screaming of a brawler with his arms pinned behind him by someone attempting to keep the peace. Immediately thereafter, he too dared to propose that "the Holy Office, in order to ascertain the truth, could conduct a test and find out whether or not Maria eats when she is taking communion."

As we already know, the ecclesiastical court could not allow itself to treat the sacraments so lightly as to use them as elements in an experiment. It is surprising, however, that Maria, lined up with other prisoners to wait for her daily half-kilo of "San Marco's bread," did not feel sufficiently sure of herself to ask that she be tested. Her failure to do so is the strongest evidence we have against her.

At this point the Holy Office, having accumulated evidence sufficient to accord Pietro Palazzi the same status as his companions, ordered his imprisonment.

21

TOGETHER FOR THE LAST TIME

*P*ietro Palazzi remained in jail for six months, during which time the inquisitor interrogated neither him nor the other two prisoners. Early in the following year, after Fra Ambrogio Fracassini was named Bishop of Pola, his brother in religion and fellow Brescian Fra Agapito Ugoni was appointed to replace him.[1] On 1 March 1663 Ugoni and his colleagues in the Holy Office decided to put an end to all the obstacles and dispatch the case.[2] The new prosecutor tried once again to reason with Palazzi and Janis, but with Don Morali he limited himself to posing the required formulaic questions.

The weaver from Zorzone responded to questions and exhortations identical to those that had been put to him before as if only a day had passed since his last interrogation. Had the defendant listened to his conscience, and was he now prepared to tell the truth which he had previously tried to hide?

"I have always told only the truth, as I am prepared to do now," Palazzi replied.

The Holy Office thought otherwise. The testimony gathered from witnesses made clear that the defendant not only knew that Maria had eaten but had collaborated in her pretense by procuring food for her. Furthermore, the woman had made fun of those who ate, "as if she were an angel in paradise, which obviously she is not. And if

1. [On Ugoni (c. 1605–74), who had spent the previous decade as inquisitor in Vicenza and would serve as inquisitor general of Venice until June 1670: see Ferrazzi, *Autobiografia*, 19, note 3.]

2. [Although long delays between interrogation and sentencing of defendants were by no means uncommon in Inquisition proceedings, it is worth noting that the new inquisitor, Ugoni, is credited in Dominican bio-bibliographies with a treatise on bringing trials to a conclusion, *Promptuarium seu elencus observandorum pro expeditione causarum S. Officii.* The present location of the manuscript of this work, which was never published, is unknown.]

such a miraculous phenomenon is to be found in the lives of a few saints among the greatest in paradise, its duration was a matter of days, not years. Those saints did not laugh at others who ate but gave thanks to God, keeping silent about the gift that the Lord God had given them." Hence Maria could not be a saint. If the defendant continued to conceal the truth about her eating, the Holy Office would have to conclude that he was in collusion with the other two "for some evil purpose or some other common interest."

Pietro Palazzi replied that the witnesses might say "what they know, or whatever they wish." He had never seen the woman eat. He had never given her any food. Nor had he heard her boast about her privilege or make fun of people who ate.

Presumably at this point the inquisitor read him the statements of his father, brother, and sister-in-law about Maria's deriding those who nourished themselves "on dirt and filth." In the peasant dialect Pietro surely recognized turns of phrase peculiar to his family, which made him change his tune. "What your Most Reverend Paternity has said is the truth, that is, that she said that we ate dirt and she didn't eat."

By yielding a bit of ground, he had stepped into a trap, as the inquisitor was quick to point out. According to what he had just said, the woman had not boasted about her privilege but had only said that she did not eat dirt like all the others. He had therefore testified falsely. While there was still time, he should acknowledge his other false-hoods. Pietro Palazzi replied feebly that it was true, she had said that they ate dirt, but only in conversation within the family.

In accordance with the rules, Maria was asked whether, before the proceedings entered the final stage, she had anything to add to what she had previously testified. In response, she expressed only two wishes, never less reconcilable than now: to reiterate the truth and to submit in obedience to the Church.

Had she eaten during the past five years?

After the trial runs in Colombo's house, she had never eaten.

The inquisitor, aware that he was dealing with pious and zealous people, had never been so patient with defendants. He exhorted her to think of her soul, for many, many witnesses had sworn that they had seen her eat.

Maria did not believe that there were so many witnesses or that they could affirm without a shadow of a doubt that they had caught her in the act. Whatever they said must relate only to her pretending to eat in order to keep her privilege secret. Only once or twice, when she was at table with strangers, had she put something in her mouth, and then she had secretly taken it out again.

How could she have kept in her mouth at least five or six mouthfuls—enough to make people believe that she was eating—and how had she got rid of them?

"I have told the truth. I haven't done these things."

No, she must respond directly to the question.

If she sat down at table, she had done so to preserve appearances, and she had taken only one or at most two mouthfuls.

One or two mouthfuls was not enough to demonstrate that she was eating like other people.

She had told the truth, and now she even doubted that she had ever been at table with others.

Given the fact that six months had passed without her deciding to put her case in the hands of an attorney, did she intend to mount a defense?

"I don't want to present a defense."

The tribunal gave her three more days to make up her mind.

Don Pietro Morali, master and guide of the little sodality of Zorzone, followed the same line as his disciples and companions, but with less firmness. "I have nothing else to say, except that I have told the truth in all sincerity, and since I have erred, I beg this Holy Office for pardon and mercy." He, too, was given three days, "so that you can prepare a written defense and do whatever else you need to do."

As the trial, scrupulously and even excessively documented up to this point, drew toward its conclusion, there are allusions to some new elements that seem to have been deliberately omitted from the transcript. We can be certain that Maria had met with an attorney, since at the end of her interrogation on 20 July 1662, she had indicated her willingness to accept the advice of counsel. "If I am assigned one or two attorneys, I shall consult with them." Perhaps she hoped that she could persuade a designated advocate to believe in her privilege. Without much hesitation or beating about the bush, the lawyer must have urged her to admit once and for all that she had eaten, just like all normal human beings. What did she have to lose? Consequently she, who from the age of eighteen on had never offended anyone, probably decided not to mount a defense, having been persuaded that the inquisitor was after all a good priest and that what she had done was a matter for the confessional, not for a lawyer's office. Thus, when, at her own request, she had come before the court on 26 July 1662, she had found herself before a tribunal in harmony with the attorney and better informed than he about celestial prerogatives.

Such a transaction with a court-appointed attorney had also occurred in the case of Don Pietro Morali, but after his initial refusal of legal assistance, he may have been informed that he would be tortured. Having faced up to this challenge, which compensated for all his former hesitations, he was not going to be frightened by one last threat, as his final statement makes clear. "I put myself in the hands of the attorney, whom I beg the Holy Office to send back to me."

In the three days at his disposal he tried again, this time more desperately, to resist the lawyer's pressure on the issue of Maria's fast, which he thought might still clear him. But it was precisely on this point, seemingly so minor and banal, that the inquisitor was least inclined to compromise—and in such a confrontation, the stronger party always wins.

An unexpected development confirms our impression that something for which there is no documentation had taken place behind the scenes. On that same very busy day, 1 March 1663, the tribunal signed a decree releasing Pietro Palazzi from prison. He was to remain under arrest, however, until someone came forward to furnish bail of two hundred ducats. He was obligated, furthermore, to refrain for the rest of his life from having any contact with Maria Janis, even by letter or through intermediaries. The third man had clearly told all or had promised to do so in a subsequent interrogation, scheduled for 6 March.

In the interim, a lawyer, Ambrogio Geroldi, made an official appearance before the court. The inquisitor gave him a copy of the transcript and ordered him to dispatch the case as soon as possible. During the same period of time, Maria and Don Pietro gave in, or simply resigned themselves to the inevitable.

But when they were brought from prison to make their final appearance in the chapel of San Teodoro, we can barely recognize the two people whom we have come to know so well, with their different but equally unbalanced reactions to their common infatuation. By promising to absolve them from excommunication, the inquisitor had either elicited generic confessions or extorted from them complete, though forced and not entirely sincere, admissions of guilt. In exchange, through the attorney, he had allowed them to save face. Nevertheless, they would manage to preserve their dignity almost intact.

Despite the well-known fact that owing to its harmonious working relationship with the civil power, the Venetian Inquisition was the most lenient in Italy, the second of these two scenarios appears the more plausible. It seems most unlikely that the Holy Office, held at bay for fourteen months by three people from the mountains who indirectly claimed faith and sacrifices greater than its own, would have renounced the satisfaction of hearing even a mentally clouded account of how and when Maria had satisfied her appetite and by what means and in what quantities her two devotees had provided her with food. This raises the disturbing hypothesis that Maria feigned also, and above all, in her confession, using her imagination to create a completely fictional account, just as her "enemies" the witches often did.

The transcript of the last interrogation of the three consists of loose pages. On 6 March Pietro Palazzi appeared before the court.

INQUISITOR: Tell us what you want to say about this matter.
PALAZZI: I say that at home in my house, having heard that this

Donna Maria enjoyed the privilege of living on communion alone, I believed it, but now I yield to the Holy Office. Also, from time to time I saw her put something into her mouth, but they told me that it was a pretense and that she wasn't eating, and I don't remember what kind of food it was. And I brought food to the house, but not for her, since they told me that she didn't eat.

INQUISITOR: How many times did you see her eat, where, when, and in whose presence?

PALAZZI: Many times, I don't remember how many, now in one place, now in another, which I don't remember, various times, in my and the priest's presence; I don't recall other people being there. Ordinarily, when there were others present, she didn't eat but rather made fun of those who were eating. ("Et se corrigendo dixit [and correcting himself, he said]") I can't say that she laughed at others who were eating.

INQUISITOR: Have you said what you have told us through hatred or through love?

PALAZZI: I've said what I've said as the simple truth to save my soul, and I beg pardon from the Holy Office.

The person who put up the bail money as a guarantee for Palazzi's release was the grain merchant Antonio Peverada, who was in contact both with Palazzi's half brother the sausage-maker and with his old father and half brother in Zorzone. To which of his two families would Pietro decide to submit? Would he return to his mountain home, where people would make fun of him as the inconvenient third person in the triangle who had been doubly duped? The one thing certain is that never again would he see Maria. For her sake he had renounced the world, and now they had persuaded him that he had betrayed God as well. In order to achieve reconciliation with Him, he would have to drive her from his mind.

From the loose sheets we can also reproduce the final interrogations of Don Morali and Maria, which also took place on 6 March. The priest was called in first.

INQUISITOR: Since your attorney has requested that you be heard, tell us what you wish to say.

MORALI: I am resolved to confess the pure truth, as I have always done. As curate in Zorzone, when Maria Janis came to me, I undertook to direct her on God's road. Having seen that she demonstrated devotion and unusual obedience, when she told me one day in church after communion that she had been called to go without eating and live on communion alone, I indulged her, exhorting her to try to live for a few days without eating. Because I observed that she had become rather weak, I urged her to eat, and many times she ate, but not because she felt the need or was hungry. On the contrary, after having eaten, she vomited up the food.

INQUISITOR: How many times a day did Maria eat?

MORALI: She ate once a day after having gone for fifteen, twenty, or thirty days without food—I'm not sure exactly how long, but more or less—fifteen or twenty days for sure. And this was at the beginning [of her real fast, following the trial runs]; before that, she went for three, seven, nine, or twelve days, longer each time.

INQUISITOR: How many times do you know that Maria ate during those five years when you claimed that she lived without eating?

MORALI: That I don't know, because many, many times I ordered her to eat, and she ate as I have said.

INQUISITOR: What has led you to confess now that Maria ate many, many times, when in all your previous appearances you persisted in asserting that she didn't eat?

MORALI: Because I have decided that I want to be certain about the state of my soul.

INQUISITOR: Tell us the whole truth.

MORALI: I really believed that she went all those days without eating, and my certainty was based on her obedience to me, because she told me everything.

INQUISITOR: Again, now that your lawyer has requested that your case be dispatched, we ask whether you wish to say anything else, since the time allotted to you for your defense has already expired.

MORALI: I say, "Mercy!," and I add that I believed what I said before, because otherwise I would not have done what I have done. And I confess that I must have been under the influence of diabolical illusion or some melancholy humor, for the Holy Office has thus persuaded me. And I beg the pardon of Lord God and the Holy Office.

Finally it was Maria Janis's turn.

INQUISITOR: Since your attorney has asked that you be heard, what do you have to say?

JANIS: I realize that before now I have not told the truth, and having examined my conscience, I am here to tell it now. I went to Zorzone, and seeing others who were under the spiritual discipline of the curate of that place, Father Pietro Morali, I joined them. And thinking that I was making progress on the spiritual path, one day the idea came to me that I could go without eating and live on communion alone, as I had heard some saints did. I conferred about this with the curate, who approved my plan. And I thought that I too could perform miracles and become, as they say, a saint. And although at the beginning it seemed to me to be a sweet thing, at the end it became very bitter. (The transcriber adds here, "Hic lugens adiunxit multa alia sicut in processu. [At this point, weeping, she added many other things that appear in the trial record.]")

INQUISITOR: Did you eat during the five years preceding your imprisonment?

JANIS: The first time, after my idea had been approved by my master, I went three days without eating, after which, because I had become weak, he made me eat. And then I went seven days without eating, and after having eaten, fasted some more. After these trials I ate many times because nature impelled me to eat, although on many occasions, through weakness, I threw up the food, which seemed like poison because I was so feeble. And during the times I wasn't eating, I lived on communion alone and purification.

INQUISITOR: How much wine did you drink in the purifications?

JANIS: Sometimes more, sometimes less, and on occasion up to half a glass, and it was the local wine, black.[3]

INQUISITOR: How long did you hold the food in your stomach before vomiting because of weakness, as you have told us?

3. [Throughout northeastern Italy, red wine is still called "black."]

JANIS: Sometimes an hour, sometimes two, sometimes half an hour with great difficulty, and sometimes I vomited immediately.

INQUISITOR: Since your attorney has requested that your case be dispatched, and since you have given up the right to present a formal defense, do you have anything else to say?

JANIS: I confess that my opinion was false, I repent, and I beg pardon of this Holy Office.

On 16 March the tribunal issued the sentences, the result of obvious collusion between the inquisitor and the lawyer. Mainly on account of his having consecrated the host and administered communion outside a church, Father Morali was judged "vehemently suspect of heresy" and condemned "to remain in a closed prison[4] for the period of five years." Maria, who had "induced" him to do so but had finally admitted that she had eaten, was, at least on the face of it, treated more leniently: she was judged "lightly" suspect of the same crime, but her sentence was to remain in jail "until the Holy Office decides otherwise."

Among the many counts against her, with which we are so familiar and which can be summed up in a single one, pretense of sanctity, Maria was even convicted of having worn clothing "made of fine fabric, unsuited to her birth and status." As far as the pretended fast is concerned, however, from our point of view she was not defeated. Even the sentence makes that clear. "Although at the beginning it seemed to you a sweet thing, at the end it became very bitter, because after you had gone for three days without eating and hence were in a weakened condition, the priest whom you called your master made you eat. And so it went on: after having eaten you went more days without food, and when nature made it necessary to take food, you ate from time to time, commanded to do so by your master, although because of your weakness you often threw up the food, which seemed to you like poison because you were so feeble." Luckily for the inquisitor, to use sporting terminology, her extraordinary ordeal did not constitute a potential world record that had to be verified.

The absurdity of her case is reflected also in the rest of the

4. [That is, in a real jail rather than under some form of house arrest.]

sentence, for the penances imposed on her amounted to a restriction of her devout life style. For five years she would have to recite the Rosary once a week, make her confession once a month, and take communion on the days set by the confessor whom the Holy Office would assign to her. In order to follow this regimen—and a person condemned for matters of conscience could hardly fail to conform to it—Maria during her long days in prison would have to struggle most of all against boredom and the ever-present temptation to do something extra for the salvation of her soul.

After each sentence came the formal abjuration, which the two convicted criminals made separately on the same day, kneeling before the Gospels with lighted candles in their hands—the exact same pose in which we saw them at the beginning of this story. In her ten-year voluntary novitiate, during which she had eaten less than the greatest of the desert saints, Maria had gained only the ability to read for herself the sentence which rejected everything she stood for.

We know nothing of the circumstances, locales, and duration of the earthly lives of the curate of Zorzone and his pupil, relatively young at the time we must leave them but already tried in their souls by the worst outcome to which their aspirations could have led them. Having widened their horizons to the greatest possible extent, they were known even in the great world, on which they had managed to have a small impact.

In the late summer of 1663 Don Pietro petitioned the Holy Office, begging that on account of the bad state of his health (attested by two medical certificates), he be permitted to move to a monastery, where he would continue his penances and "to some extent earn his bread." His great faith in God and in his fellow men had not deserted him, and as usual, it was extended to his colleagues in religion. He assured the Holy Office that the Franciscan friars of San Francesco della Vigna had offered to take him in out of charity. The tribunal granted his petition, but not before having obtained a security deposit of five hundred ducats from one Cristoforo Orsetti, a prosperous Bergamasque merchant accompanied to court by two witnesses, a fellow countryman who held a responsible position in the Arsenal and the ubiquitous Antonio Peverada. Two weeks later, however, the guarantor was forced to return to the Holy Office and request that he himself be permitted to provide asylum for the condemned man, assuring with the large sum put on deposit that the man would never leave his house in Venice, because the reverend fathers of the monastery "had not shown themselves willing to receive him."

The beginning of Maria's new life was more obscure and mortifying. During the summer the ecclesiastical tribunal acted for the last time on her case, granting her the favor, which she had not requested, of being transferred from jail to "the pious establishment of the Mendicanti of this city, provided that the governors of that place consent to receive her."

They certainly would have received her: men like humility, and when the Holy Office made a recommendation, it could not be debated.[5] In that house of refuge for beggars and derelicts, which was probably harder to get out of than prison, Maria Janis of Vertova must have finished her days.[6] Her social status did not afford her the luxury of protectors or friends prepared to guarantee her good conduct. After all, as the reverend fathers of the Inquisition had succeeded in demonstrating, she was only a woman.

5. [In fact, Maria's name does not appear in the minutes of meetings of the governors of the Mendicanti, preserved in the archive of IRE (Istituzioni di Ricovero e di Educazione) in Venice.]

6. [Neither Janis's nor Morali's name appears in the necrologies kept by the Provveditori alla Sanità (Venice, Archivio di Stato) between 1663 and 1700, but there are many gaps in this series.].

ENCOUNTER WITH A
MANUSCRIPT

In June 1976 I submitted to my editor the manuscript of my novel *La miglior vita,* which was inspired by my perusal, both stimulating and traumatic, of the death registers of the parish church in my native village, Giurizzani.[1] I then began to explore Lutheranism in Istria, a partly spontaneous development subsequently given impetus and direction by Pier Paolo Vergerio, the apostate Bishop of Capodistria,[2] and other philo-Protestant Istrian priests: Baldo Lupetino and his distant relative Mattheus Flacius Illyricus of Albona, Stipan Consul of Pinguente, Anton Dalmatin, and Primus Trubar, the last three of whom established the written languages and literatures of Croatia and Slovenia.

My initial interest in this subject stemmed from a piece by Pier Antonio Quarantotti Gabini, published posthumously. The Capodistrian writer had argued that during the Reformation era our border region "revealed something of its true character ... The sixteenth century was the first critical moment in the soul and mentality of Venezia Giulia, the only moment in which we didn't follow but rather led the way for the other regions of Italy."[3] Not long thereafter I read

1. *La miglior vita* (Milan: Rizzoli, 1977).

2. I subsequently explored the career of Vergerio in *Il male viene dal Nord: Il romanzo del vescovo Vergerio* (Milan: Arnoldo Mondadori, 1984).

3. "Pagine inedite di Pier Antonio Quarantotti Gambini," introduced by Riccardo Scrivano, *Trieste,* n.s. 20, no. 97 (April 1975): 17–39; quotation from p. 30. [By "Venezia Giulia," a term coined in 1863 by the philologist Graziadio Ascoli, Quarantotti Gambini meant not only the territory now included in the Italian provinces of Gorizia and Trieste, but also the hinterland of Trieste and the Istrian peninsula, which passed after World War II, via the London Memorandum of 1954 between Italy and Yugoslavia (reaffirmed in the Treaty of Osimo in 1975), to Yugoslavia. Today the official meaning of the term covers the provinces of Gorizia and Trieste, which, together with the provinces of Pordenone and Udine, comprise the Regione Autonoma Friuli-Venezia Giulia, established in 1964. *Guida d'Italia: Friuli Venezia Giulia,* 5th ed. (Milan: Touring Club Italiano, 1982), 107–9.]

Carlo Ginzburg's fascinating study *Il formaggio e i vermi,* which among other things underlined the penetration of Protestantism into the nearby region of Friuli, although the author made clear that the beliefs of his protagonist, the miller Menocchio, were largely his own personal creation.[4]

In the Biblioteca Civica of Trieste I found the early volumes of an Istrian scholarly journal which published a list of all the natives of Istria and Dalmatia tried by the Venetian Inquisition and extracts of the trials of several heretics from Dignano (near Pola).[5] Then, in the Archivio di Stato of Venice, which holds the records of that Holy Office, I was able to pursue my investigation of the Protestant group in Dignano, which was inspired by master artisans and even priests and their sons, all men of Greek origin who had immigrated to the Venetian coast of Istria following the occupation of their homeland by the Turks.

These documents fully confirmed Gambini's insight. Those master artisans, only partially literate and without expert guidance, who risked (and sometimes lost) their lives by reading a vernacular edition of the Bible in secret and disseminating their views, manifested a rebellious spirit fueled by a genuine thirst for truth and knowledge— one never before nor since expressed so vigorously by my fellow Istrians. Listen, for example, to what witnesses testified about two shoemakers, father and son. "Andrea Calegaro, standing at his window and seeing a woman on her way to light a lamp in honor of the Madonna of Fasana, told her that she'd make better use of that oil by dressing a salad." "[He said] that confessing to any Tom, Dick, or Harry was just as good as confessing to priests, because they were men like anyone else, and that it wasn't necessary to make one's confession to anyone other than God, because the priests had no more authority than ordinary layfolk to absolve sins." "[He claimed] that some fucking cuckold pope who had sardines to sell and couldn't find any customers had invented Lent." "[He asserted] that it would be better to find husbands

---

4. [See Introduction, page xii, note 3.]

5. (La Direzione), "Processi di luteranismo in Istria," *Atti e memorie della Società istriana di archeologia e storia patria* 2, fasc. 1–2 (1886): 179–218; 17 (1901): 150–86, 283–99; 18 (1902): 44–74, 248–73; 19 (1903): 35–55; 20 (1904): 46–77, 283–329. The list is in the first installment of this article.

for the nuns so that they would have babies and the population would increase and multiply." "He despised the images of the saints and said that they were like masks." "He said that holy orders were bogus, that holy oil was worthless, that confirmation was nothing, that the sacrament of penance was nothing." Here we see the ideas and the spirit of the Reformation, which had filtered into the region of Italy most exposed to northern influences, and which, at least in Dignano, were promulgated by immigrants of Greek Orthodox origin, particularly ill-disposed toward the Church of Rome.[6]

The nineteenth-century manuscript index to the records of the Venetian Inquisition in the Archivio di Stato of Venice[7] includes not only trials against Protestants conducted in the second half of the sixteenth century but also innumerable prosecutions from the seventeenth and eighteenth centuries of those offenses against the Catholic faith most common in the preindustrial world: "witchcraft,"[8] fortune-telling, abuse of the sacraments, ecclesiastics' keeping concubines, seduction in the confessional, and so forth. I decided that once I had completed my research on Dignano, I would take a look at a trial that had attracted my interest: the proceedings against one Maria Iani or Jani of Vertova, whose offense was categorized as "pretense of sanctity." In the published list of cases against natives of Istria and Dalmatia which I had consulted earlier, Vertova was followed by a question mark, since the anonymous com-

---

6. The fruit of this research—completed after the present book—is *Quando Dio uscì di chiesa: Vita e fede in un borgo istriano del Cinquecento* (Milan: Arnoldo Mondadori, 1987).

7. [Indice 303: Sant'Uffizio was compiled between 1868 and 1870 by Giuseppe Giomo and Luigi Pasini.]

8. [*Stregherie*, the word used in the trials as well as in Index 303 of Venice, Archivio di Stato, is a pejorative term for casting spells in order to win (or deprive someone else of) health, love, or money. Recent research has shown that witchcraft in the classic sense—making a pact with the Devil and participating in orgiastic ceremonies with him (the Witches' Sabbat)—was a relatively minor feature on the Italian, and particularly the Venetian, scene. See, for example, Ruth Martin, *Witchcraft and the Inquisition in Venice, 1550–1650* (Oxford: Basil Blackwell, 1989); Romano, *Inquisitori* (full citation in chapter 18, note 2); and Anne Jacobson Schutte, "Donne e pietà nel Seicento veneziano," forthcoming.]

piler knew of no locality of that name in our territory.[9] Nevertheless, reluctant to let anyone from our region slip through his patriotic net, the careful scholar had opted to include the case against Jani, a surname not uncommon in Istria. The place name which had puzzled him sounded vaguely familiar to me: I wondered whether it might be linguistically related to the names of two hamlets, Verteneglio and Petrovia, not far from my native village. More than simple curiosity about exactly where between Trieste and Spalato a place called Vertova might be found piqued my interest in the misfortunes of that Maria. I recalled another Maria, a distant relative of mine who had emigrated to Latin America before I was born. She had come back a couple of times to make known to us not only her religious devotion (which by then had assumed a markedly Hispanic cast) but also her gifts as a healer and exorcist, learned as a child while she tended flocks on the Carso[10] and perfected, perhaps, under the tutelage of some Indian woman in the New World.

Since I had just finished creating an ideal village sacristan torn between the decidedly superstitious religiosity of his peasant neighbors and the doctrine dispensed by parish priests (some exemplary and others less so), this seventeenth-century trial interested me for two other, more substantial reasons. In the trials I was reading, I was encountering the Holy Office as it pursued its original aim, the elimination of Protestantism. Besides seeming remote in time, the Dignano trials presented what was in effect a group protagonist—an unmitigatedly positive one because of the defendants' unswerving commitment to their beliefs—the members of the local elite assailed by what was in effect a foreign culture. I felt myself drawn toward the second, more complex phase of the inquisitorial enterprise and toward a more clearly delineated individual protagonist.

Hence, halfway through my research on the Dignano group, I ordered the file on my "countrywoman" of long ago who had been put on trial for allegedly feigning sanctity. A glance at the cover page revealed the error committed by the compilers of the manuscript in-

9. "Processi di luteranismo," first installment, p. 215. Clearly the anonymous compiler of the published list had examined the trial itself rather than relying exclusively on the manuscript index, in which the defendant's place of origin is given as Bergamo.

10. [The rocky ridge that extends from west of Trieste into Istria. See *Guida d'Italia: Friuli Venezia Giulia,* 17–18, 21, 194–99.]

dex in the Archivio di Stato and repeated by those who published the list of Istrian and Dalmatian defendants: they had omitted the final s from the name of the woman put on trial, which had persuaded me as well as the Istrian scholars of the late nineteenth century that she must have come from Venezia Giulia. In fact, Maria Janis came from Vertova in the diocese of Bergamo, which then was part of the Venetian Republic; she had been sentenced on 16 March 1663 along with the priest Pietro Moralli (or Morali), her curate and master.[11]

As I began to work my way through the 250 manuscript pages, which I had considerable difficulty in deciphering, the story of Maria Janis and Pietro Morali, a sort of love affair transported onto the spiritual plane, struck me as extraordinary, bordering on the paradoxical and the grotesque—but at the same time strangely familiar. There's hardly a village in which people don't recount the scandal of the priest who left town with his favorite female parishioner. Before long, however, it became clear to me that although Don Pietro and Maria had lived together in an attic apartment in one of the most obscure corners of Venice, a district of ill fame, their purpose was to cultivate their own form of contact with the divinity. They were in such a close relationship with God that they kept Him with them and fed on Him whenever they wished in the form of the bread which the devout woman conserved between her breasts. In that double, sacrilegious intimacy they were discovered by their curious neighbors and, via the women's confessor, denounced to the Holy Office.

From the first interrogation on, the two prisoners expounded the confused principles (sometimes, though they did not realize it, in competition with those of the Protestants) that had inspired their doctrine and their even more eccentric way of life. The woman had allegedly lived for five years on communion alone, and her escort, also in odor of sanctity, saw his function as being to serve as an unimpeachable (as it turned out, an overly credulous) witness. Besides recording the declarations of the two zealots from the mountains, the transcript revealed a panorama of seventeenth-century life that stretched from

11. Venice, Archivio di Stato, Sant' Uffizio, busta 110, dossier entitled "*15* [*sic*] *Martij 1663. Expediti fuerunt Presbiter Petrus Moralli et Maria Janis, Diocesi Bergomensis.*

their miserable parish of Zorzone between the Val Brembana and the Val Seriana, the scene of their Sunday exploits, all the way to Rome and Venice, where the odd couple ventured in order to make known Maria's incredible "privilege," but in which they did not dare to move too far away from the familiar ambience of countrymen who had moved to the cities to better their economic and social status.

Even before becoming completely absorbed in this vivid and strange affair, I was impressed by the sharp contrast between the ideas and principles enunciated before the tribunal by Janis and Morali and those I was encountering in trials conducted less than a hundred years earlier. It appeared to me that in the peasant world, in other respects so immobile over the course of centuries, the campaign of the Counter Reformation had produced a reversal in the ethical priorities, and particularly in the consciences, of a population conditioned for the most part by the eternal return of the seasons. An effective way of documenting this inversion, I think, is to juxtapose some statements made during the Dignano and Morali-Janis trials.

Andrea Calegaro of Dignano d'Istria "ridiculed and laughed at" those who went to church and often claimed "that it's not what enters through the mouth that fouls a man, but rather what goes out." Maria Janis of Vertova "laughed at and made fun of us who ate and said that it was shameful to eat; she also said that food was dirt and filth, and that one mustn't enjoy oneself while eating and forget God." Andrea: "These sheep who go to receive the host thinking that it's the body of Christ—the fools don't realize that it's just a little dough made with flour." Maria: "Always, from the time I was a little girl on, I've had a special affection and reverence for the most holy sacrament, and when possible I have always tried to go to mass and take communion. One day, some time after I had submitted myself totally to the will of God, the idea came into my heart that I mustn't eat or drink any longer, because it was an ocean of infinite love."

Here we have two mental orientations which involve two opposite natures and inform their respective modes of expression and life styles. Keeping pace with movements of revolt and restoration, they have alternated over a millennium of Italian history until today, when they coexist—on the surface, explicitly and proudly separated, but underneath, very often cunningly combined. Let me put it more explicitly. The vast majority of Italians, precisely those in the vast underclass, who like Maria Janis found themselves forced to brand their souls with guilt for loose living and privileges they in fact never enjoyed and who were excluded from the great intellectual leap forward of the Enlightenment (only to suffer the reversion of the nineteenth century), have never recovered from the repression and the thoroughgoing, fervent reorganization of the Catholic Church which followed the Council of Trent and culminated in the seventeenth century. Our vision of the world, our choices of life styles, our perceptions of the victories and defeats that accompany them, the anxious search for conciliation and hence for protection, the anticipation of special favors, even the little or extraordinary expedients for evading this internal servitude or escaping from it once and for all: every one of them is the consequence of the phobias and fanaticism of the Counter Reformation. Like it or not, that is our most genuine heritage. The novel that reflects it best remains *I promessi sposi*, the great fictional creation that ends in the year and region in which our chronicle begins. Although I had no such intention, the story I have told, because it remains faithful to the sources, comes close to constituting a refutation of Manzoni's literary account, which it counters with a harsher, less comfortable, and still current reality: the cruel conditions of life in the fields, the process of urbanization and consequent deracination, the sense of alienation which leads to the only refuge possible, that of faith, often a new source of frustration rather than comfort, into which our protagonist plunges with an enthusiasm disproportionate to her cultural level, ending up by remaining captive to it like a drug addict. We can also recognize the modernity of her story in the odd contribution that it brings from the age of the Counter Reformation to the Freudian paradigm. In addition to the compensatory or self-punishing dreams of Maria, consider her totally sublimated love for Don Pietro, symbolically consummated in the carnal act through the rite celebrated in the Venetian attic, after which the two feel obliged to remake the bed.

I have just alluded to the Italy of the late twentieth century. In the two kinds of trials mounted to expose and punish two distinct forms of heresy, one external to the Church and the other born within it as the consequence of a mutation or an overly violent blow, it is not difficult to recognize two contrasting rationales for repression, certainly less legal, that is practiced today on various continents. In both types, we find summary or deliberately trumped-up proceedings, fabrication of insufficient and arbitrary evidence and testimony, physical and mental torture, brainwashing. Those charged, whether they stand firm or collaborate to the point of self-critical recantation, emerge not only condemned but also offended in their faith or betrayed in their trust. It doesn't much matter which rationale has been more prevalent in the twentieth century, since in both cases the direct aim of the prosecutors—to wound consciences—has been achieved.

Considerations of this sort, on my mind as I struggled through the transcript of the trial against Maria Janis and Don Pietro Morali, further stimulated my interest in the case. Finally the matter took complete hold of me, unfolding as an unexpected love story and even as a sort of religious detective story, full of suspense and *coups de théâtre*. (There was even a "third man" or super-witness, who ended up in jail; it was the sister who betrayed the defendant.) What came to the surface above all, however—enough for me to draw away for the first time from my geographical confines and immerse myself in a long, ahistorical infancy—was something else. Peasants, who at first sight appear almost subhuman, in fact reveal themselves through their speech. Perhaps for that very reason, literary treatments of them that put words into their mouths are almost inevitably distorted. When we listen to them talking, we learn that peasants were both resigned and wild, depressed rather than brutal, often loyal, occasionally kind, sometimes hopeful despite the fact that in their world the slow passage of time was marked by the tolling of funeral bells: "There were four little girls and boys, but only one of the boys lived."

In the record of the trial, furthermore, I found a cast of characters so familiar and at the same time so contradictory—Don Morali, for example, wavering and stubborn, cautious and reckless, always loyal and always disobedient—as to stimulate irony, filter out naive sentimental partisanship and emotional involvement, and give rise at some points to bitterness and disappointment. Indeed, my greatest worry during the deciphering of the manuscript and the spontaneous reconstruction of an episode whose course resembled a spiral, now arching upward, then turning back on itself to regain momentum, stemmed from my apprehension that Maria's total abstinence, insisted upon by her devoted Pietro Palazzi in unison with her confessor, Pietro Morali, would turn out to be merely a shabby imposture. Instead, all the evidence so painfully gathered and passionately mustered to expose her seemed inconsequential and irrelevant in the face of the tenacity with which the woman from Vertova, starting out from the centuries-old misery of her native environment, attempted to mount the ladder leading straight to paradise. Living in an era of religious emulation rather than of authentic mystical fervor, she was certain that sainthood was the counterpart of a feudal privilege extended to the humble, which was attainable through the renunciation of material needs and of human nature itself.

She might have managed to convince even me that for five years, without interruption, she had not touched food. A fascinating treatise by the sixteenth-century writer Simone Porzio, which concerns a German girl whose long fast was observed and verified by a physician,[12] encouraged me to believe that such a phenomenon could have repeated itself in the damp cellar of Zorzone. But in my heart of hearts, I came to realize that what I really admired about Maria was her fashioning of the alleged pretense, which presented her with a challenge even greater than the sacrifice of not eating. It is precisely this creation, necessary under the circumstances and confirmed at some points in the trial record by unimpeachable evidence, that promotes her in historical hindsight to a higher class than her humble origins enabled her to attain during her lifetime.

Readers may well ask whether I accept the explanation that Maria was simply faking. My response is negative. Strengthened by the burden of a renunciation—not continuous but still extraordinary— the woman from the mountains of the Bergamasco occasionally found herself unable to pursue her exclusive communion with God. In order to return to Him, she believed herself entitled to take the liberty of nourishing herself. Although in those moments God did not choose to support her, she was confident that He would not judge her according

---

12. *Disputa dello eccellentissimo filosofo M. Simone Portio Napoletano, sopra quella Fanciulla della Magna, la quale visse due anni e più senza mangiare e senza bere,* trans. Giovanni Battista Gelli (Florence: [Lorenzo Torrentino], 1551?).

to human standards. On the contrary, sooner or later, He would justify her to His representatives on earth. But in the end God did not bestir Himself, and her superiors, like all those on earth who hold any kind of authority, could not stand having it challenged. Thus, through the irony of history, the small degree of recognition that, three centuries later, this book accords to Maria Janis is due not to her holiness but rather to her humanity.

Appendix: Seventeenth-Century Money

Doppia (*doble*): a gold coin minted in Italy and Spain; its Venetian weight was fixed during the reign of Doge Francesco Erizzo (1631–46) at 6.806 grams (twice the value of a *scudo* or *zecchino*).

Ducato (ducat): not the classic Venetian gold ducat, first minted in 1284, but a silver coin introduced in the first decade of the seventeenth century, when the *zecchino* replaced the old ducat. In the 1660s it was minted in two forms, the *ducatone* (weighing 28.103 grams) and the *ducatello* (weighing 23.4 grams).

Giulio: a silver coin first minted during the pontificate of Julius II (1503–13) which weighed between 3 and 4 grams. There were eleven *giulii* in a *scudo d'oro*.

Lira: a silver coin weighing 6.25 grams; there were 16 *lire* in a *zecchino*.

Paolo: a silver coin first minted during the pontificate of Paul III (1533–49), identical in value to the *giulio*.

Scudo: a gold coin minted in the Papal States (see *giulio* above) and elsewhere, roughly equivalent in value to the Venetian *zecchino*.

Soldo: a mixture of silver and other metals weighing 2.039 grams; there were 120 *soldi* in a *zecchino*.

Zecchino: a gold coin, first minted in the early seventeenth century to replace the old *ducato;* during the reign of Doge Domenico Contarini (1659–74), it weighed 3.494 grams. It was coined in abundance during this period, both because silver was in short supply and because this particular denomination was well accepted in the eastern Mediterranean, where the Venetian Republic was engaged in the War of Candia against the Turks.

SOURCES

Martinori, Edoardo. *La moneta: Vocabolario generale.* Rome: Multigrafica, 1977.

Papadopoli Aldobrandini, Nicolò. *Le monete di Venezia.* 3 vols. in 4. III.1. Venice: Libreria Emiliana, 1919.